ADVANCE PRAISE FOR

Voices in Black
Political Thought

"The principal strength of Ricky K. Green's work is that he offers accessible means to think about, discuss, understand, and analyze immeasurable complexity. One of the major findings of Black scholarship over the past half century is the almost infinite complexity of the lives of African peoples. That scholarship has revealed a world so varied, complex, and dense that there are no precedents for how to think about it productively. Professor Green provides a pathway to understanding a central aspect of this nexus—the centrality of Black culture in Black political conceptualizations and actions, at both mass and elite levels. This is an area of thought so convoluted, contradictory, and wide-ranging that an intellectual short-hand is required to make sense of it. In an extraordinary intellectual tour de force, Professor Green has provided it."

David Covin, Professor Emeritus of Government and Ethnic Studies,
Immediate Past President, the National Conference of Black Political Scientists

Voices in Black
Political Thought

AFRICAN AMERICAN LITERATURE AND CULTURE

Expanding and Exploding the Boundaries

Carlyle V. Thompson
General Editor

Vol. 7

PETER LANG
New York • Washington, D.C./Baltimore • Bern
Frankfurt am Main • Berlin • Brussels • Vienna • Oxford

RICKY K. GREEN

Voices in Black
Political Thought

PETER LANG
New York • Washington, D.C./Baltimore • Bern
Frankfurt am Main • Berlin • Brussels • Vienna • Oxford

Library of Congress Cataloging-in-Publication Data
Green, Ricky K.
Voices in Black political thought / Ricky K. Green.
p. cm. — (African-American literature and culture; v. 7)
Includes bibliographical references and index.
1. African Americans—Politics and government. 2. African Americans—
Intellectual life. 3. African Americans—Social conditions.
4. African American intellectuals. 5. African American philosophy.
6. Political ethics—United States. 7. African diaspora.
8. African Americans—Historiography. I. Title. II. Series.
E185.G756   973'.0496073—dc22   2004005484
ISBN 0-8204-7299-9
ISSN 1528-3887

Bibliographic information published by **Die Deutsche Bibliothek.**
Die Deutsche Bibliothek lists this publication in the "Deutsche
Nationalbibliografie"; detailed bibliographic data is available
on the Internet at http://dnb.ddb.de/.

Cover design by Dutton & Sherman Design

The paper in this book meets the guidelines for permanence and durability
of the Committee on Production Guidelines for Book Longevity
of the Council of Library Resources.

© 2005 Peter Lang Publishing, Inc., New York
275 Seventh Avenue, 28th Floor, New York, NY 10001
www.peterlangusa.com

Printed in the United States of America

Contents

Black Political Morality

Haunting Voices: Introduction

Here in America, in the few days since Emancipation, the black man's turning hither and thither in hesitant and doubtful striving has often made his very strength to lose effectiveness, to seem like absence of power, like weakness. And yet it is not weakness—it is the contradiction of double aims. The double-aimed struggle of the black artisan—on the one hand to escape white contempt for a nation of mere hewers of wood and drawers of water, and on the other hand to plough and nail and dig for a poverty-stricken horde—could only result in making him a poor craftsman, for he had but half a heart in either cause.[1]

Political stasis is the existence of a deep chasm between two essential competing forces within a society. Such a chasm inhibits political development within the society.

Du Bois' problem of double aims reconstructs the experience of political stasis within the Black context. Black people in the United States currently endure a political stasis. The source of that stasis was revealed more than one hundred years ago in W.E.B. Du Bois' statement above—the double aims of the Black artisan. From time to time the stasis shrouds itself within other conflicts, and those concerned about the lack of political development in the Black community, to quote Du Bois, turn "hither and thither" attempting to shore up the dike with anxious fingers, arms, and sometimes with their lives. There indeed have been monumental efforts and a parade of heroic children, women and men; still the consensus of most Black people is that to date, the Black community has yet to fulfill its political potential and there is much more fundamental work to be done before past efforts can be recognized as successful.

Our crisis of political stasis is consistently cast as a failure of leadership. Du Bois' quote above focused on leadership, as did his political philosophy. Over the century, a host of commentators have followed suit. Nearly a hundred years after Du Bois, in the aftermath of yet another White-cop/Black-youth shooting, in the aftermath of yet another tragic inner-city rebellion, a frustrated and angry Cincinnati Black youth echoed, in a more negative and angry tone, Du Bois' focus:

> Our Black leaders are not leading us. Some of our black leaders just want their faces on TV. They are in this for four things only: reputation, power, politics and money.[2]

Both arguments, that of Du Bois and our youth, reveal, at least in the Black context, that the crisis of stasis is a crisis of identity, both individual and collective identity. Black leaders, even if they found themselves morally fit to lead a population desperate for excellence in leadership, would find the task nearly impossible.

Harold Cruse, in his monumental work, *Crisis of the Negro Intellectual*, identifies the inability of Black leaders to understand and operate within the constraints of Black culture as the most essential problem of Black politics. Cruse argued that the crisis of Black identity was truly a crisis of culture. *Crisis* reconstructed a fundamental conflict between the intellectual elite and the working class they sought to politically mobilize. The conflict began with elites' inability to understand, participate in and utilize Black working-class culture on the most fundamental of political levels.

Since Cruse completed his work, that conflict, which Du Bois envisioned as our double aims, has developed into a deep schism. That which predominates within Black communities is a plethora of oppositional discourses and competing institutions. This is the substance of Black political stasis—the competition between elite discourses and institutions over the resources of the Black community. That competition has been, at critical moments, harsh and brutal. It is a competition that Anglo American institutions don't understand and are ill equipped to deal with on even the most basic of levels.

Another key to the political stasis and the proliferation of questionable Black leadership results from the propensity of Black intellectuals to analyze Black politics, Black culture, Black thought, Black experience, indeed Blackness itself as if Black people were passive agents within their own context. This severely constrains Black political morality, and narrows its scope and function. This propensity to analyze Black culture as a passive agent is a propensity that neither Du Bois nor Derrick Blassingame, our Cincinnati youth, share with these intellectuals.

The final key results from the lack of strong mediating institutions and discourses within the Black community. This paucity exacerbates the crisis in identity that the community endures. What is lacking is a functional, effective, Black political philosophy. The historical difficulty of Black communities to produce significant and lasting mediating discourses and institutions, contributes directly to two inter-related problems—the aforementioned predominance of oppositional political discourses within the community and the absence of strong motivating forces to persuade individuals and institutions to reconcile their interests to community interests. This often produces, as our Cincinnati youth asserts, self-interested, inadequate, undisciplined, and frustrated Black leadership and politics.

Alternatively, there exists in the Black community a deep well of intellectual energy, diverse and dynamic, nurtured within an environment rich with alternative discourses. In fact, much can be gained in an environment rich with strong, active, political discourses engaging one another *within the context of community.* Political stasis dominates the environment exactly because there exists within the context of community no equally energetic and dynamic mediating discourses or institutions to moderate and assist in the development of such an environment. And while Black intelligentsia consistently attempt to reconstruct democratic discourses and analyze democratic institutions within the Black community, such attempts will continue to be lacking without recourse to strong discourses and/or institutions that serve a mediating function. The ability to reconcile individual interests to community interests forms the initial building block of democracy. Du Bois recognized this in his critique of Black leadership; we can do no less.

So we find ourselves between distinct alternatives—b'twixt and b'tween, as some would have it. On the one hand, we need to develop a fuller understanding of Black political morality. On the other hand, we need to restrain ourselves from excessively constraining a deep, rich political discourse. To resolve our dilemma, we turn to Black culture. Black people in the United States have developed a distinct culture. Our dilemma as a political phenomenon emanates from within this distinct culture and has developed within this distinct culture. As Cruse so succinctly informs us, it is only within Black culture that we shall be able to reconstruct the discourse to resolve our dilemma.

One of the clearest articulations of Black culture appears in Lawrence Levine's *Black Culture and Black Consciousness.* Levine's work is essential because it articulates and analyzes this experience on a variety of levels. These levels go beyond the ideological political strategies that most commentators on Black politics and Black culture find essential. Levine's articulation and analysis of the development of Black consciousness contributes to an understanding of Black political morality exactly because he demonstrates that the Black consciousness is distinct, deliberative and selective. Black culture represents for Levine more than a series of ideological strategies against White racism, capitalism and other forms of oppression. It is a series of conscious choices about what a distinct group of people experience as morally essential within a particular environment and beyond any particular environment.

> To argue that Negro secular song has functioned primarily or even largely as a medium of protest would distort black music and black culture. Blacks have not spent all of their time reacting to whites and their songs are filled with comments on all aspects of life. But it would be an even greater distortion to assume that a people occupying the position that Negroes have in this society could produce a music so rich and varied with few allusions to their situation or only slight indications of their reactions to the treatment they were accorded. While black secular song is not dominated by such reactions, it is a rich repository of them and offers a new window onto the lives and into the minds of a large segment of the black population.[3]

There are, however, complications with such a methodology of understanding Black political experience. One of the most significant complications also emanates from within Black culture. For centuries, Black people have utilized a unique medium to develop Black culture. Narratives, often called hidden transcripts, are at the core of Black political discourse within the United States. For that reason, reconstructing Black culture, especially in regards to political thought and action, becomes exceedingly difficult.

The first problem is that of access. Can all members of the group have potential access to the complete pantheon of cultural meanings at critical moments? One would be hard pressed to construct a positive argument concerning universal access to all facets of Black culture. The second problem is that of institution. Institution is a more concrete and much more burdensome problem for contemporary Black political morality. Can a community developing in a hostile environment institute in a functional way a culture that has developed from narratives and/or hidden transcripts?

We may begin our inquiry into Black political morality by attempting to gather, synthesize and understand Black voices from within the cultural context. This methodology is based in no small part on Levine's work on Black culture and Black consciousness. Levine's methodology in looking at Black culture achieves many essentials. We turn to Levine, not necessarily because he provides us with any direct solutions to our question, but because he, better than any student of Black culture including Du Bois, articulates the conflict of stasis at the most essential level concerning Black political morality: the level of existence. Du Bois' articulation primarily concerns individuals, and by way of Du Bois' particular focus, individual Black elites. Levine's work operates on the level of culture:

> As the outside culture became more visible and accessible in the twentieth century, the dilemma grew. The *lames* might be laughed at within the group, but it was they who often

had the better chance of mobility and success outside. Negro children were hardly socialized to the vernacular of their own group before they learned of its disadvantages and low
status in the larger culture. Thus for black Americans as for other minority groups in the
society, the socialization process increasingly became a dual one: an attempt to learn to live
both within and outside the group. In language as in so many other areas of black culture
this has produced a broad and complex spectrum.[4]

In fact, Levine's work offers the strongest support for Du Bois' theory of double consciousness on the collective level. The work is unique in that Levine does
not necessarily attribute class undercurrents to this schism, as do other writers. The
schism can produce class differentials, but class mobility is not the only impetus for
action. The most essential impetus, in fact, lies within the hierarchy of Black cultural values, which may not necessarily place class mobility in a place of prominence. For Levine, much like Du Bois, the double consciousness is a cultural
phenomenon.

At this point we can begin to link the double consciousness with political
morality and begin to develop a strong Black political philosophy. Black philosophy, strong Black philosophy, offers us a tool to analyze and articulate both problem and possible solution:

> A reading of the thinkers included in this anthology suggests an initial characterization of
> philosophy within this tradition as essentially an intellectual power of *mediation*. It is the
> philosopher's role, for example, to mediate the desires and expectations of the individual
> with the interests of the collective, interests that the philosopher will be quick to acknowl-
> edge are themselves largely responsible for the particular contour of the individual's desires
> and expectations.[5]

If Hord and Lee are correct, then Black political philosophy is uniquely situated
and responsible for understanding *and* mediating the schism within the Black
double consciousness. To achieve this, Black political philosophy must delve into
the "hidden transcript," the Black oral tradition, deep into our cultural voices. We
then must reconstruct a democratic tradition that can be developed into an understanding of political morality and instituted on a fundamental level. This, no less,
is what we have been tasked by Derrick Blassingame, and strangely enough, by
Du Bois himself, although from different times and spaces within the Black
experience.

Conceptual Voices: Methodology

These words sank deep into my heart, stirred up sentiments within that lay slumbering, and
called into existence an entirely new train of thought. It was a grand achievement, and I
prized it highly. From that moment, I understood the pathway from slavery to freedom. It

was just what I wanted, and got it at a time when I least expected it. . . . The very decided manner with which he spoke, and strove to impress upon his wife with the evil consequences of giving me instruction, served to convince me that he was deeply sensible of the truths he was uttering. . . . What he most dreaded, that I most desired. What he most loved, that I most hated. That which to him was a great evil, to be carefully shunned, was to me a great good, to be diligently sought; and the argument which he so warmly urged, against my learning to read, only served to inspire me with a desire and determination to learn.[6]

Black political morality, the political morality of people of African heritage in the United States and other areas of the African Diaspora, is distinct, culturally defined and culturally experienced. Although this assertion may initially appear straightforward, it is extremely controversial. The controversy exists in the intellectual conflict over whether or not Blacks throughout the Diaspora share elements of a common culture and whether or not Blacks within the United States share a common culture. Without recourse to a common culture, arguments that assert Black political morality as a distinct experience are severely constrained, weak whispers in the face of prevailing winds.

This inquiry attempts to present a preliminary understanding of Black political morality within the context of Black culture in the United States. While the major emphasis is not to systematically prove the existence of Black culture, we must necessarily begin to expose the contours of Black culture to begin to uncover a historical and developmental understanding of Black political morality. As with any other culture and political morality, Black political morality is inherently linked with Black culture. Both fundamentally develop and ultimately operate upon the level of existence. To expose the contours of one experience is to begin to expose the contours of the other. Indeed, I will presently venture, especially to detractors of Black culture, that in order to disprove the existence of Black culture, they must first disprove the existence of a distinct Black political morality.

To begin to define political morality, one must first realize that all systems—governing, educating, religious, social, etc.—contain both a hierarchical component and a moral component. The two possible exceptions—exceptions we have severe reasons to question, since humanity has yet to record a sustained example of their occurrence—are anarchy and nihilism. At any rate, political morality may best be conceptually defined as the synthesis of spiritual, historical and analytical thought that develops, maintains and governs human activity. As a general guide, one may argue that the political paradigm in the Untied States developed within the Lockean tradition, with extensive components of thought derived from Aristotelian and Platonic traditions. I bring this up to illuminate two points. First, any political morality can simultaneously embrace divergent, even contradictory, traditions of thought. Second, despite diversity, each tradition is interpreted through the lens of Anglo American political and moral history, or, more precisely, the history it cares to develop and retain. This latter phenomenon allows collectives distinctiveness and focus in the area of political morality.

Black political morality in the United States develops from an amalgamation of African cultural traditions and adaptation of fragments of European traditions, primarily Anglo American traditions. Adding to this complexity is the fact that while Black political morality has some access to these older traditions, it develops from and helps to maintain a cultural tradition that is distinct from either the amalgamation of African cultures or the adaptation of European fragments. This new tradition at present is one that is, relatively speaking, clearly defined and historically accessible.

Historical accessibility predominates and strongly defines Black political morality as a hierarchic and value-seeking experience. Black people within the Diaspora can *intellectually* trace their moral and political origins and development with few problems and a significant degree of subtlety. In fact, the average Black person within any Diaspora community can, if pressed, give a reasonable account of Black political history beginning with the upheaval caused by the slave trade. Most Blacks are also aware of the development of moral and hierarchic values and principles within their community in reaction to that upheaval. The development and maintenance of Black political morality spans generations. Those generations are conscious of that development and maintenance as a historical experience. They know that their understandings are, and will be, "handed down." Generations of conscious group development, the conscious development of political and moral understandings, argue the existence of culture.[7] For Black people within the Diaspora, a significant portion of this development has been handed down through oral traditions. Indeed I will argue that oral traditions are most significant, not for recording history, but for developing understandings of Blackness through the development of a unique political philosophy.

Achievement and resistance form the two most essential aspects of political morality. What makes a political morality unique is the relationship between achievement and resistance. In liberal capitalism, for example, resistance is predominantly experienced as a group concept, while achievement is predominantly experienced as an individual concept. In contrast, we can envision a communist or socialist political morality where the concept of achievement is experienced primarily as a group concept. The group-versus-individual predominance that we speak of may be an allusion at this point in our inquiry. The more significant observation is that in liberal capitalism, individual achievement is left fairly unconstrained; while in other political moralities, individual achievement could be, and often is, much more severely constrained. One could argue, probably with significant success, that in liberal capitalism, individual achievement is the prioritized goal (and we shall soon come to see this in connection to liberal-capitalist understandings of freedom). Other political moralities may prioritize group resistance in relation to individual achievement.

Existence, the will to survive, forms the immediate foundation of resistance. The primary impetus for resistance can be shown to be emotion/instinct. That emotion/instinct operates as a balance to humanity's environment, which constantly threatens the existence of individuals and the collective. The emotion/instinct can range from anger at those things that threaten existence to joy for those things that enhance existence. This emotion/instinct operates upon a scale from immediate, sometimes temporary, sometimes intermittent emotions, to long-term, nearly permanent, emotions/instincts. On the immediate end of the scale we could place anger, joy and pleasure. On the more permanent end of the scale we could place will, and desires such as reproduction. More dynamic emotions/instincts such as love and hate could fall anywhere on the scale from permanent to temporary.

The emotions/instincts at the immediate end of the scale form resistance to the dynamics of the environment—wild animals, other predators including other humans, catastrophic events, volcanoes, monsoons and wars that humans encounter and produce within any specific environment. The emotions/instincts at the permanent end of the scale form resistance to the human condition. Births, injuries, illnesses and most notably deaths—those states that are inevitably part of humanity's cycle of existence. The more dynamic emotions/instincts form resistance to the human condition as it interacts with the environment. For example, love is not necessary for reproduction and it may not even lead to reproduction, but in particular environments it is a significant quality sought by individuals attempting to reproduce and may even be valued above the process of reproduction.

We could argue that resistance is an individual phenomenon. However, to do so places resistance within an alien context. To be complete, resistance must operate on the collective level. It is only on the collective level that resistance can operate as a normative value in regards to states such as death. To our knowledge, no individual has successfully resisted the state of death. It is only through collective action that we can make sense of death as part of the human condition. Resistance therefore exhibits a strong collective component.

The will of human beings to survive requires the development of at least a bare concept of morality. Not only is it essential for humans and other entities to survive, that survival is also reasoned, must be reasoned, as good. The thought of existence being a necessary good reinforces the priority of the emotions/instincts of resistance. These emotions/instincts become the initial foundation of spiritualism.

The will of human beings to survive also requires the development of at least a bare concept of equality. That bare concept must operate between individual and environment and among individuals alike. As thinking animals, humans must not only develop the instinct to survive, they must think that their survival is as essential as the survival of all else within the environment. In this context, we must resist the capacity of the environment and our fellow human beings to end our existence. Resistance concerns relationships among equals—all have an equal capacity to exist and to seek continued existence.

Achievement, as a component of political morality, is linked to the concept of control. Achievement is individual and/or collective success in *controlling* the self, the collective and the immediate environment. The idea of actually being able to control oneself, the collective and/or the environment is ultimately an ideal. However, the ideal is the goal. The goal is often conceived as excellence, virtue or order.

There are two different types of excellence that pertain to achievement. The first type of excellence is internal, the excellence of mastering oneself—one's emotions/instincts. This type of excellence is achieved through the development of rational thought as a system of constraint. The second type of excellence is external, that of mastering other human beings and the environment. This is achieved through acquisition, competition and imposition of order.

In most political moralities, internal excellence has priority. In other words, most political moralities argue that in order for one to control others and the environment, one must first learn to control oneself. So the ability to control is first conceived of as an ordering of oneself. This ordering has often been conceived of as an ordering of the soul, or psyche, in which desires are given low priority and therefore severely constrained, spirit is given a somewhat higher priority but still closely constrained, and rational thought is given the reins and left unconstrained except by its function of controlling and ordering the other parts of the soul (*Republic*, 329a–354b). As lower functions, the desires are quickly equated with the physical world and the control of the body.

Internal control is a transition between resistance and external understandings of achievement. It is shrouded in the same emotion/instinct that shrouds resistance. One sees this in the writings over the entry to the temple of Delphi—*know thyself, nothing in excess, curb thy spirit, observe the limit, hate hubris, bow before the divine, fear authority, glory not in strength*. In fact, the Oracle at Delphi represents that transitional period in Greek development between resistance as the main function of the *polis* and the rush to develop empire.[8] In many ways we should envision Christianity as fulfilling the same function. The framers of the U.S. Constitution understood this phenomenon, and their understanding resonates through the provision of the Constitution that provides for the separation of church and state. The provision operates as a defensive mechanism, protecting individual rights through the First Amendment, but in addition, access to the broader concept within the spirit of U.S. government allows a government to clearly separate resistance and external manifestations of achievement. The crux of the argument is that while most political theories consider internal control most essential, most societies consider, once they establish their sovereign power, external control to be most essential, as it allows them to control and exploit their environment.

Achievement is not a relationship that assumes or considers equality to be essential. It is an inequitable, internalized, relationship that requires individuals to objectify their environment and other entities that are part of that environment, *including other human beings and themselves.* Achievement envisions and creates relationships between entities that are inherently hierarchic.

The current concept of achievement popular in the United States, which includes the contemporary system of distributive justice (merit), develops in Western political thought from the ancient Greek concept of *agon*, which signified contest or struggle:

> The Greeks tended to judge people not on a "pass or fail" criterion, but by deliberately imparting a competitive character to as many aspects of life as possible (e.g., plays, songs and dances at festivals), and the wide difference between the treatment of winners and the treatment of losers augmented the incentive to excel.[9]

The struggle or contest concerned excellence; in an environment politically dominated by men (as opposed to nature, animals, slaves and women), excellence and merit was determined through inequitable relationships between the individual and other entities. Fourth-century Athenian orator Demosthenes (lxi 52) articulates the essence of this competitive experience:[10]

> If you are better than those whom you encounter, do not cease trying to excel everyone else too; consider that your aim in life should be to become foremost of all, and that it is more to your advantage to be seen to aim at that eminence than to appear outstanding in ordinary company.

While there has always been a strong individual component to achievement, it is nonetheless a group-defined and group-driven phenomenon. Standards of and rewards for achievement are set by the needs and desires of a particular group. Ironically, achievement, as Demosthenes argues, is an activity that ultimately requires individual and group to go beyond constraints, both environmental and societal. The ability, the necessity, to transcend constraints fulfills the widest and deepest understanding of achievement. In its foremost state, achievement is the most aggressive and competitive activity of human individuals and human associations.

The relationship between achievement and resistance within Black political morality is constrained by the polar experiences of slavery/dehumanization and freedom/cultural development. The importance that is placed on these experiences distinguishes Black political morality among other political moralities throughout history. Black resistance *and* achievement develop, as the Douglass quote at the beginning of this argument indicates, within experiences that are inherently revolutionary in relation to Western civilization. Because both develop out of revolutionary experiences, their relationship in its correct context is rooted in revolution. Douglass' meaning should not be trivialized. What Douglass is arguing is that Black self-determination, the basic attempt of a group of people to determine for themselves the principles and values upon which their lives and their children's lives should be based, is a revolutionary idea in Western thought.

Because it is a revolutionary idea relative to Western thought, the source of Black political morality, Black culture, has to be situated as radically different in relation to Western European culture. Even in its most progressive form, Western European culture does not have the resources, analytical or historical, to support the consistent development of a political morality that must not only challenge, but must overcome, essential Western values, principles, institutions and history.

This work, then, does not fit into the scope of a critique of race-based politics in the United States, nor is it a mere commentary upon politics (race based or otherwise). On the other hand, neither is it an empirical study of Black culture. It is a work with the primary concern of reconstructing a discourse that can mediate between competing understandings of Black political morality. To achieve this function, it relies upon three distinct methodologies. First, primarily through the medium of history, it attempts to gain an understanding of culture as a foundation for the development of political morality, political thought and political action. Second, primarily through the medium of political science, it attempts to uncover the source of stasis—competing understandings of Black political morality and thought—within Black culture. And finally, through the medium of political philosophy, it attempts to reconstruct a discourse of mediation to bridge these competing understandings.

Consequently there are three distinct types of works that form the primary research for this manuscript. The first type, obviously, is works that provide an understanding of the development of Black culture. The second type is works that provide an understanding of Black political conflict. The third type consists of works that provide an understanding of Black morality, including Black spiritualism. Readers are cautioned that within the discourse, especially early within the discourse, these three methodologies are not envisioned as separate components by particular authors. In fact, their ability to not separate, or alternatively to bring together these component parts, whether intentional or not, contributes to the excellence of these works.

The first work that stands as a foundation for the development of our understanding is one that falls in the above category. Frederick Douglass' group of works: *The Narrative of the Life of Frederick Douglass: An American Slave; My Bondage and*

My Freedom; and *Life and Times of Frederick Douglass* provide us with a glance into the early development of the culture of Black people held in bondage. Douglass' works, which are written as autobiographies, expose us to a particular understanding of Black culture. As one of the most ardent anti-slavery advocates of his age, Douglass tended to dichotomize Black culture between intense resistance:

> Every tone was a testimony against slavery, and a prayer to God for deliverance from chains,[11]

and extreme submission:

> It was deemed a disgrace not to get drunk at Christmas; and he was regarded as lazy indeed, who had not provided himself with the necessary means, during the year, to get whisky enough to last him through Christmas. From what I know of the effect of these holidays upon the slave, I believe them to be among the most effective means in the hands of slaveholder in keeping down the spirit of insurrection.[12]

Douglass' dichotomy provides us with an excellent understanding of Black culture as resistance to dehumanization. He is one of the few writers of his period who is able to provide us with a firsthand account of the development of resistance on the cultural level.

Douglass' immediate successor in this regard proved to be W.E.B. Du Bois, whose work, *Souls of Black Folk*, while considered less academically sound than *Black Reconstruction*, is much more revealing in regard to the development of Black culture. *Souls* looked at Black culture from a perspective of historical development, and as the title of the first chapter suggests, it envisioned that development as a striving toward acceptance within the human community. In some real sense, Du Bois attempted to heal Douglass' dichotomy, bringing together the best elements of the component parts of the Black community:

> He would not Africanize America, for America has too much to teach the world and Africa. He would not bleach his Negro soul in a flood of white Americanism, for he knows that Negro blood has a message for the world. He simply wishes to make it possible for a man to be both a Negro and American. . . . [13]

Maybe more essential was Du Bois' attempt to develop a democratic discourse out of this double consciousness. In fact, for Du Bois, Black people held the key to the survival and development of democracy within the United States. In *Souls*, while the philosophic premise approaches excellence, support for the premise rests upon Du Bois' problematic understanding of Black culture, an understanding grounded in the problematic concept of race:

> To put it more simply: sharing a common group history cannot be a criterion for being members of the same group, for we would have to identify the group in order to identify its his-

tory. Someone in the fourteenth century could share a common history with me through our membership in a historically extended race only if something accounts for their membership in the race in the fourteenth century and mine in the twentieth. That something cannot, on pain of circularity, be the history of the race.[14]

While I agree tentatively with Appiah's critique of Du Bois in the area of race, such a critique only functions in the case of race and only when philosophy is prioritized over and above politics. What Appiah has ignored is that groups do not have to be *naturally* created. If in fact any group is "natural," it is not due to any genetic markers but because association is "natural" or common to humanity. So the fact that race is "socially constructed" simply means that the most essential factor in determining group membership is agreement of a collection of individuals— either explicit or tacit agreement. Such criterion is political *and* philosophic in nature. A mere philosophical critique as Appiah presents cannot do away with the concept of shared history. In other words, sharing a common group history can be criterion for being members of the same group exactly because we have identified the group and its history. The fact that we, someone in the fourteenth century and myself, share a common history is exactly because we will it, or as Du Bois put it, because "of our spiritual strivings." Since we have taken a leap of faith, Appiah's problem of circularity is irrelevant to the creation, development and maintenance of our group and its shared history. What may be more significant for our inquiry is the fact that due to a strict interpretation of Western philosophy and a passive understanding of Black history, Appiah seeks to deny us what other populations have developed as a matter of necessity—self-determination.

My only disagreement with Du Bois in this area is that because the concept of race can be externally imposed against the will, the concept of culture is more appropriate, more democratic and more revealing in the sense that it does not allow scholars to analyze the political thought and action of Black people as inherently passive. Culture operates simultaneously upon the philosophic level and the political. It not only allows our will to develop a group identity out of a shared history, since history is a discipline, it also allows those who do not share that history an exit. This exit enhances democracy because it is self-imposed and as such, to the greatest extent available, definitive. This is where Du Bois' *Souls* attempts to take us—to the development of a democratic discourse out of the striving of double consciousness by choice as well as necessity.

C.L.R. James' work on revolutionary Haiti, *The Black Jacobins*, shared similar goals and a similar methodology. However, the culture of focus was not based upon a dichotomy of consciousness, but instead was based upon an amalgamation of African cultures and their will to create a common history. Their success provides us with a glimpse at a Black Diaspora culture that developed to the point of sovereignty, or successfully adapted a particular environment to its will—within human understanding. James' work is limited in the same manner as Du Bois'. Despite the development of the concept of "new Blacks," the work is grounded in the problematic concept of race. It is not that this concept was not operative upon the revolutionary discourse of Haiti, it is that the use of such a concept obscures the more essential philosophic conflict that James approaches excellence in uncovering—the development of a Black philosophical tradition that transcends the social construction of race while simultaneously engaging oppressive aspects of a political moral hierarchy grounded in the Western political tradition.

Harold Cruse's work, *Crisis of the Negro Intellectual*, was the first significant work that attempted to address the shortcoming of race and replace the concept with culture as the most significant foundation of Black politics and Black political thought. Cruse's work was monumental in exposing the double consciousness as the source of failure in Black leadership:

> As long as the Negro's cultural identity is in question, or open to self-doubts, then there can be no positive identification with the real demands of his political and economic existence. Further than that, without a cultural identity that adequately defines *himself*, the Negro cannot even identify with the American nation as a whole . . . *thus it is only through a cultural analysis of the Negro approach to group "politics" that the errors, weaknesses and goal failures can cogently be analyzed and positively worked out.*[15]

Cruse's work grew out of the cultural awakening that was known as the Harlem Renaissance and became one of the first works to energetically analyze the problem between Black Integrationists and Black Nationalists. Still the crux of the work was centered upon the concept of cultural identity. Cruse's problem, however, remained similar to Du Bois' problem in that Cruse functionally could not expose the contours of what he called Black culture, although he did expose the conflict that marked the development of Black culture.

A decade following Cruse's publication, Lawrence Levine, in his work *Black Culture and Black Consciousness*, addressed the shortcomings of Du Bois, Cruse and James with an exhaustive study of Black culture. Levine's work is significant in bridging the gap between Black culture and Black political thought because Levine was able to examine and articulate an understanding of the development of Black culture within a particular political environment. He was able to show both how a culture resisted and adapted to aggressive demands and how such a culture developed its own aggressive agenda to adapt the environment to its needs.

Levine exposed political contours by looking into the development of Black culture in stark detail. His attention to the practical as well as the philosophical allows one to envision the development of politics, and ironically, Du Bois' double consciousness on the cultural level:

Thus for black Americans as for other minority groups in the society, the socialization process increasingly became a dual one: an attempt to learn to live both within and outside the group. In language as in so many other areas of black culture this has produced a broad and complex spectrum.[16]

However, Levine's work suffered on the opposite end of the spectrum than did the work of Cruse and Du Bois. Levine, a historian, exposed the relationship between politics and culture primarily due to the fact that his writing dealt with a culture developed in political conflict and mired in an intensely dynamic political environment. While the outline for developing a democratic political thought is present in his work, it never develops much beyond the outline.

The work that to date has come the closest to achieving a complete understanding of the relationship between Black culture and Black politics has been Robin Kelley's *Race Rebels*. *Race Rebels* is a study of what Kelley and others call the "infrapolitics" of the Black working class:

. . . I use the concept of infrapolitics to describe the daily confrontations, evasive actions, and stifled thoughts that often inform organized political movements. I am not suggesting that the realm of infrapolitics is any more or less important or effective than what we traditionally understand to be politics. Instead, I want to suggest that the political history of oppressed people cannot be understood *without* reference to infrapolitics . . . [17]

The fact that infrapolitics can only be implemented on the cultural level justifies Kelley's methodology of studying politics from "way, way below" as an accurate synthesis between the cultural and political. Such methodology is revealing in the sense that it uncovers that, at least for the Black population in the United States, critical political development can begin on the collective level and be transmitted throughout the group without the implementing force of traditional political institutions. Kelley's study of key Black political spaces—such as dance halls, and even mobile spaces such as buses—as places in which infrapolitics develop and flourish, exposes Black culture and Black politics as much more radically dynamic and democratic processes than previously articulated. In one sense, Kelley fulfills the promises of Du Bois' *Souls*. In another sense, the need to show Black cultural politics as a mediating and moderating influence between conflicts, Kelley fails. In fact in regard to the conflict most essential for Kelley, the conflict between the Black working class and emerging Black middle class, *Race Rebels* tends to solidify the classes and exacerbate the conflict between them.

This then is our beginning—the attempt to envision culture as not just fertile ground for the development of political morality but also the very terrain out of which develop the discourses and institutions of political mediation. We wish then to uncover both the political and the philosophical aspects of Black culture and determine how they have developed and in which ways they have assisted and can continue to assist in the mediation and resolution of conflicts within the Black community.

The remainder of this work is organized in the following manner. Chapter Two is an inquiry into the development of Black political morality. It seeks specifically to uncover the parameters of the relationship between resistance and achievement in the Black community. It takes a look at the initial stages of development of three distinct strains of Black thought through a cultural and textual analysis. Chapter Three presents an analysis of the development of resistance within Black community. It seeks to uncover how that development has been instituted on various levels, especially on the level of culture and how that institution has affected the development of Black political thought within the context of the three strains. Chapter Four presents an analysis of the development of achievement within the Black community. It seeks to uncover how achievement has been instituted upon various levels, placing a special stress on the cultural level. It also reconstructs the development of the three strains of Black political thought into three distinct traditions. Chapter Five is concerned about the development of fragmentation within Black political morality. The chapter places the impetus for that fragmentation within traditions competing for resources within the community. It places the conflict between institutions primarily concerned with resistance and institutions primarily concerned with achievement at the center of the stasis. The final chapter looks to the development of Black political thought as the possibility of a solution for the stasis. It is concerned with the experience of mediation as the foundation of Black political philosophy and looking at the possibility of the development of a strong discourse of mediation and in turn institutions of mediation within the Black community.

Cultural Thought

The notion of sacredness gets at the essence of the spirituals, and through them at the essence of the slave's world view. Denied the possibility of achieving an adjustment to the external world of the antebellum South which involved meaningful forms of personal integration, attainment of status, and feelings of individual worth that all human beings crave and need, the slaves created a new world by transcending the narrow confines of the one in which they were forced to live. They extended the boundaries of their restrictive universe backward until it fused with the world of the Old Testament, and upward until it became one with the world beyond. The spirituals are the record of a people who found the status, the harmony, the values the order they needed to survive by internally creating an expanded universe, by literally willing themselves reborn.[1]

It is to Black culture we must now turn to understand the unique way Black people within the Diaspora develop, maintain and utilize the experiences of resistance and achievement. The truth is, once we tear away the various veneers atop most definitions of culture, we find that culture represents a tool for individual and group survival and development. In fact, the widely accepted definition of culture as a "people's way of life," intimates at least the survival aspect. More conservative definitions of culture such as "the best a people produce" intimate the developmental aspect.[2]

Nothing within reason or history prevents a particular group of people from consciously grounding their survival and consequently their culture upon a foundation of political necessity. In other words, Black people throughout the Diaspora exist within an environment where politics and economics are and always have been the predominate factors concerning their survival and development. Black culture nurtures an acute political and economic awareness on both the individual and group level. This may well be an extremely difficult concept for those who stand outside the culture to comprehend.[3] After all, there are so many other facets to life, so much more for individual and group to achieve. The key to understanding Black existence is the ability to envision the Black experience as a striving from political and economic weakness to political and economic strength. The necessity and development of this striving form core concerns within Black thought.

African cultures throughout the Diaspora survived the movement of African and European peoples into the Western Hemisphere. Within the Diaspora, the degree of fragmentation of African cultures caused by the movement and oppression of African peoples was not uniform but varied, dependent upon environment. Black people in the United States developed a specific and distinct culture in response to a distinct and particular type of slavery. Resources retained from Africa (cultural paradigms, fragments and strands) proved essential to this development. Black culture is not externally created, imposed or developed. It is a reaction to the environment based upon African fragments and the understandings they engendered.[4] Black people in the Diaspora share a distinct historical paradigm that is constantly utilized in the gathering and processing of political and moral information. The Black experience in the United States is just one variant within that historical paradigm.

Black cultural uniqueness proceeds from the historical development of tools, the main purpose of which is to assist individuals susceptible to specific environmental dangers to resist and transcend these dangers. As tools of culture, achievement and resistance both develop within the historical experience concerned with protecting *individuals and the collective* from oppression. The ultimate function of achievement and resistance is directly related to understanding and transcending hybrid racial/economic oppression, dealing with the most essential environmental threat. The other part of that uniqueness is that Black culture itself recognizes a deficiency in the area of achievement. For over two centuries, the stress in Black political morality has been in collective resistance. That stress has necessarily placed critical constraints upon achievement, especially individual achievement—we should readily recognize the constraints upon individual Black leaders being demanded by our Cincinnati youth (see Chapter One, FN 2). Why shouldn't leaders seek power, money and reputation? Such ambition is part of the American liberal tradition. The answer is straightforward even if somewhat complex. Black culture must construct an understanding of achievement that takes into consideration understandings, experiences and traditions that developed from over two centuries of resisting systems of achievement founded upon Black dehumanization and later maintained upon the premise of Black inferiority.

Black political morality is the ranking of those tools of survival and development within the context of resistance and achievement. It is a ranking exactly because we rate tools in order of their ability to bring about our conception of something, not without considerable hesitation, that can only be labeled as the good of the community. This chapter posits that the foundations of Black political morality predominantly developed—from the fragments of various African cultures—during the period of resistance to, and endurance of, dehumanization throughout the entire Diaspora including the United States. This development took place within three distinct types of Black communities: free Black communities in states that outlawed slavery early, Maroon communities in which fugitive slaves congregated, and communities in which Black people were still held in bondage until the aftermath of the Civil War. Three distinct strains of Black thought initially develop out of these three distinct communities. Those three strains approached the question of dehumanization from distinct perspectives. Due to the longevity of the experience of dehumanization and the resistance required to address it, these communities each developed their own unique relationship between the experiences of achievement and resistance.

Fugitive Voices

What we need to immediately concern ourselves with is the contours of Black political morality. How do we begin to sort out an understanding of Black political morality from the various acts of the people of the period we are concerned with? Such is a monumental and, to some extent, arrogant task. Where we might begin our search is with Black activity in opposition to the institution of slavery. If slavery constituted a dehumanizing institution, then it is there that the prolonged struggle of Black people of the Diaspora begins; there, within the cracks and crevices they discovered, that Black people began to reconstruct and develop a unique systematic understanding of humanity. Reacquiring and maintaining one's humanity in the face of such an institution as Western European racial slavery would represent the initial foundation for reconstructing and developing a political morality in a new environment.[5]

The writings and speeches of Frederick Douglass, more than any other Black political thinker during the period, grapple with the conflicts inherent in this problem. Douglass, who liberated himself from bondage, understood and fiercely articulated that the first step toward freedom entailed the reconstruction of one's humanity. It is in this struggle for humanity, articulated by Douglass and other enslaved Black people, that the foundations of Black Diaspora culture develop. These foundations constitute an articulation of a Black political morality—an initial ranking of the essential feelings, principles and values of Black people.

That ranking is both typical and surprising, and what it has to say about the human condition is enlightening. Existence held the first and foremost position in the ranking. However, we must be careful when defining existence. For Blacks within the Diaspora, there were various levels of existence, and priority was often given to the sanctity of mental and/or spiritual existence as opposed to the physical. Resistance, as the second priority, flowed from the experience of striving to exist. A critical experience of existence is the striving toward equality, which also becomes a necessary experience of resistance. We must remember the complexity of Black political morality and understand that for Blacks within the Diaspora resistance to slavery was ultimately experienced as resistance to dehumanization. Black people, obviously, resisted slavery and dehumanization ultimately to achieve freedom. However, they did not necessarily prioritize physical freedom in relation to other components of life such as family. Family occupied a critical position within Black political morality. More often than not, family proved to be the most essential impetus for resisting dehumanization.

Douglass and other Blacks held in bondage bring this ranking to life within context. To understand this context, one must begin with the question: "What exactly were Blacks held in bondage after?" Lewis Gordon, in the opening essay to his edited volume on Black philosophy, *Existence in Black*, frames the question in the following manner: "Why do they go on?" To begin to answer that question through the voices of Blacks held in bondage, one must be patient enough to uncover and listen to those voices:

> I was quite a child, but I well remember it. I never shall forget it whilst I remember anything. It was the first of a long series of such outrages, of which I was doomed to be a witness and a participant. It struck me with awful force. It was the blood stained gate, the entrance to the hell of slavery, through which I was about to pass.[6]

Douglass writes of the first time he witnessed the beating of his aunt Hester, "a woman of noble form, and graceful proportions," by his old master, Captain Anthony. Douglass is concerned with the immorality of Anthony and the pain suffered by Hester. Douglass' work is primarily a critique of slavery. But within that critique, we find answers to our questions of Black existence:

> He had ordered her not to go out evenings, and warned her that she must never let him catch her in company with a young man, who was paying attention to her belonging to Colonel Lloyd. The young man's name was Ned Roberts, generally called Lloyd's Ned.[7]

> Aunt Hester had not only disobeyed his orders in going out, but had been found in company with Lloyd's Ned; which circumstance, I found, from what he said while whipping her, was the chief offense.[8]

Hester braved the warnings of Captain Anthony to spend time with the young man, Ned. Despite the constraints placed upon self-determinant Black action, Black people sought out those moments in which they could naturally (unconstrained by the process of dehumanization) express the joy and experience the pleasure of their own human existence.

> Nor did he ever suggest that he was different from other slaves in this respect. He believed that all slaves came naturally to the conviction that they should be free. . . . The slaves' natural conviction that they should be free was also the reason why the slaveholders treated them so cruelly.[9]

Boxill's concentration on freedom in his analysis of Douglass is both revealing and limiting: revealing in the sense that it allows him to articulate the universal nature of resistance among those held in bondage; and limiting in the sense that by concentrating on freedom, in lieu of dehumanization, it develops a false dichotomy that causes the focus of the work to be somewhat skewed. Freedom is only one aspect of humanity—a very fundamental aspect, still only one aspect. By focusing on the natural inclination of those held in bondage to find and assert their humanity, we can begin to develop a broader and deeper analysis. It is this inclination, the need of Blacks held in bondage to find and assert their own humanity, that draws the cruelty of their oppressors.

Douglass assists us in this area with his periodical insights into the psychological influences of slavery. Douglass is writing a critique of slavery with the main function of ending the institution. His critique offers us an argument that is a synthesis of politics and philosophy. Most often he grounds his argument in negative observations. The first essential observation deals with the slaves' detachment from their own birth, which Douglass announces as the ignorance of most slaves of their birth date.[10] The second essential observation is where Douglass takes us from the few moments he had occasion to be with his mother, her death early in his life and the lack of emotions associated with her passing.[11] The third observation is where Douglass analyzes his connection to his brother and sisters. His claim is that the relationship between his siblings and himself is for all intents and purposes nonexistent due to his mother's death. For this reason, when he is sent by himself to Baltimore to begin the second stage of his bondage, he looks forward to leaving the plantation where he grew up.[12]

At that point in his life, Douglass estimates that he was probably between seven and eight years old.[13] His detachment from any conception of a nuclear biological family, and the experiences that come with such conceptions, is nearly complete.

It is this moment in his narrative that Douglass exposes to his readers the mind-set that spent more than three quarters of a century pursuing freedom and equality for himself and other Black people. What Douglass begins to unveil to us is that he values that which can bring him closer to his goal of freedom and disparages that which cannot. Nowhere is that more evident in his choices of friends and enemies.

Douglass, like most orphans and many detached slaves, struggles to construct for himself a surrogate family of Black people (and sometimes Anglo Americans) who share or can assist him in the acquisition of his pursuit. This is the first institution, an experience of family that sometimes incorporates blood relationships but often transcends those relationships. This experience of family is common throughout the Black Diaspora. Conceptually, it is an experience that borders on the concept of community. Douglass' particular family is founded upon his desire to be free, his particular form of resistance to the institution of slavery. Other families were founded upon blood relationships and/or the necessities of plantation existence. These institutions formed the initial foundation of Black culture and it is in these institutions where Blacks begin to develop the value system of political morality. It is in these institutions where forms of resistance other than individual freedom take precedence:

> Fannie Moore also remembered that her mother often suffered from "trouble in de heart" over the way she and her family were treated on the Moore Plantation after so many years, and "every night she pray for de Lord to get her and her chillen out of de place." One of the main reasons why conditions were so horrible, according to Ms. Moore, was the fact that Fannie's mother continually resisted any brutal treatment of her children.[14]

> The master, Billy Grandy, whose slave I was born, was a hard-drinking man: he sold away many slaves. I remember four sisters and four brothers; my mother had more children, but they were dead or sold away before I can remember. I was the youngest. I remember well my mother often hid us all in the woods, to prevent master selling us. When we wanted water, she sought for it in any hole or puddle formed by falling trees or otherwise: it was often full of tadpoles and insects: she strained it, and gave it round to each of us in the hollow of her hand. For food, she gathered berries in the woods, got potatoes, raw corn, &c. After a time the master would send word to her to come in, promising, he would not sell us. But at length persons came who agreed to give the prices he set on us. His wife, with much to be done, prevailed on him not to sell me; but he sold my brother, who was a little boy. My mother, frantic with grief, resisted their taking her child away: she was beaten and held down: she fainted; and when she came to herself, her boy was gone. She made much outcry, for which the master tied her up to a peach tree in the yard, and flogged her.[15]

The struggle to form the most basic human institution, the family, relied heavily upon spiritualism. As Levine's quote at the beginning of this chapter posits, spiritualism performed an essential function within the community whether it was expressed in terms of Christianity or other traditional forms of African spiritualism:

> I found Sandy an old adviser. He told me, with great solemnity, I must go back to Covey; but that before I went, I must go with him to another part of the woods, where there was a certain *root*, which, if I would take some of it with me, carrying it *always on my right side*, would render it impossible for Mr. Covey or any other white man, to whip me.[16]

By essential function, we might consider that Black spiritualism informed and was infused in every experience:

> I did not, when a slave, understand the deep meaning of those rude and apparently incoherent songs. I was myself within the circle; so that I neither saw nor heard as those without might see and hear. They told a tale of woe which was then altogether beyond my feeble comprehension; they were tones loud, long, and deep; they breathed the prayer and complaint of souls boiling over with the bitterest anguish. Every tone was a testimony against slavery, and a prayer to God for deliverance from chains.[17]

This experience was made richer and deeper through the medium of the soul:

> The hearing of those wild notes always depressed my spirit, and filled me with ineffable sadness. I have frequently found myself in tears while hearing them. The mere recurrence to those songs, even now, afflicts me; and while I am writing these lines, an expression of feeling has already found its way down my cheek. To those songs I trace my first glimmering conception of the dehumanizing character of slavery. I can never get rid of that conception. Those songs still follow me, to deepen my hatred of slavery, and quicken my sympathies for my brethren in bonds.[18]

It is within Douglass' two passages above that we can experience the true function of the spirituals and the effectiveness of the medium of music. Douglass writes plainly enough of the spirituals as a testimony against slavery and a prayer to God for deliverance from chains. Because Douglass is so true to his calling, he reveals to us another, maybe more profound, function of the spirituals—the defining, development and maintenance of the Black community. Douglass, who in many ways, admittedly, exists only peripherally as a member of the community of bondage, especially at the time when he wrote *Narrative*, is still held by the collective feeling that the spirituals engendered.

The spirituals and Black spiritualism, as part of Black resistance, tended to level the community, to foster throughout the community of resistance a distinct understanding of equality. One found it hard to live through the selling, punishment and mistreatment of one's offspring, one's siblings, one's friends or even mere acquaintances of the Black community without the deep feeling that Douglass experiences, without meeting those abusive actions with some form of resistance. Mother cannot endure the selling of a child without herself experiencing the cruelty of the plantation owner. Sandy Jenkins, who must counsel Douglass to returning to Covey, cannot do so without feeding the youth, putting his family in danger and finally revealing to the younger man a root of protection. Futile efforts? Or attempts to spiritually cleanse the way for loved ones we cannot physically protect? The latter can only be done through attempting in some manner to lift another's burden.

Again Douglass does miss some of the intricacies of the Black community because of the unique circumstances of his early years and his intense focus on *physical* freedom. Because Douglass expends much energy, he almost slips past the importance of spiritualism to the community and individual. As Levine intimates, devoid of the traditional means of building community, Blacks held in bondage achieved community through spiritual means. In attempting to understand the Black narratives, we should begin to recognize the clarity with which Douglass, Moore, Grandy and other Blacks held in bondage communicate concerning the resistive acts of their parents, especially their mothers. Douglass, while despairing over the early loss of his mother, remembers with stark clarity the burden she bore to visit him those few times before her death. Moore and Grandy remember intimate details of such burdens concerning their mothers. It is through resistive acts such as these mothers endured, that the Black family developed and survived the period of bondage. Though child and mother may have been separated by the plantation owner's economic pursuits or plain cruelty, it is doubtful that even the inhumanity of the systematic bondage experienced in the Southern United States could erase from a child the picture of a parent struggling against all odds to maintain the institution of family and community.

The spiritualism of resistance not only served an egalitarian leveling function within the community; it attempted to extend that function to relationships between its members and those of the oppressive community. Though Jenkins counseled Douglass to return to the plantation, the contribution of the root is meant to protect Douglass from further beatings—not simply to allow him to endure the beatings but to prevent the beatings from ever occurring again. Fannie Moore's mother's prayers were for her children's freedom. Mose Grandy's mother hid her children and even her misplaced trust in the plantation owner is indicative of the hope of equality:

> Not only did slaves believe they would be chosen by the Lord, there is ample evidence that many of them felt their owners would be denied Salvation.[19]

Blacks in bondage used spiritualism to create and maintain a semblance of equality between themselves and their oppressors.

The attempt to define and implement equality through spiritualism was the first step toward the development of a physical equality. Douglass alludes to this over and over again in *Narrative*:

> I may be deemed superstitious, and even egotistical, in regarding this event as a special interposition of the divine Providence in my favor. But I should be false to the earliest sentiments

of my soul if I suppressed the opinion. I prefer to be true to myself, even at the hazard of incurring the ridicule of others, rather than to be false, and incur my own abhorrence. From my earliest recollection, I date the entertainment of a deep conviction that slavery would not always be able to hold me within its foul embrace; and the darkest hours of my career in slavery, this living word of faith and spirit of hope departed not from me, but remained like ministering angels to cheer me through the gloom.[20]

It is not only Christian spiritualism that fuels Douglass' desire for physical freedom. In a somewhat revealing, somewhat cryptic passage, Douglass, that same morning after receiving the "root" for protection from Sandy Jenkins, becomes embroiled in a battle with Covey that he deems life-changing.[21] As Douglass writes, the root was fully "tested" as the sixteen-year-old battled the more experienced Covey for his life. Douglass prevailed, getting what he believed was the better of the fight. The fight did much more for Douglass:

> The battle with Mr. Covey was the turning point in my career as a slave. It rekindled the few expiring embers of freedom, and revived within me a sense of my manhood. It recalled the departed self confidence, and inspired me again with a determination to be free.

One of Douglass' many commentators, Boxill, questions Douglass' early commitment to nonviolent resistance or moral suasion.[22] But for Douglass and most Blacks held in bondage and those recently free, the depth of spiritualism required for resistance is lasting. Douglass' early reliance upon nonviolent suasion—until he becomes totally frustrated with it as a method to facilitate Black freedom and redeem Black humanity—is part of the Black experience. More than a century later, we see the same phenomenon in Martin Luther King Jr. and even in the more radical El Hajj Malik El Shabazz. It should not be taken as part of slave mentality or worker docility as many commentators have alleged. Instead this spiritualism is the foundation of, as Levine argues, a "rebirth" and the rebirth the foundation of Black resistance.

The deepest, most revealing answer to our initial question of what Black people held in bondage were after is that they wanted out of hell, as they envisioned slavery. While many like Douglass were able to become fugitives, most found relief in family and community, and the resistive acts centered within these institutions. For both of these groups there were sacrifices: the first group, in detaching themselves, most often sacrificed family and/or community for freedom; the second group, in attempting to root themselves, sacrificed physical freedom. While popular belief in the area of study has asserted that the faction between field workers held in bondage and house workers held in bondage was the most deep-seated conflict within the emerging Black community, the split between these two groups, those able to detach themselves from community and those able to sacrifice individual freedom for community, quietly offers the deepest seeds of conflict within an emerging Black political morality. The conflict is not necessarily antagonistic, nor oppositional, though it is a source of tension. The tension exists between the necessity to continually develop, adapt and refine institutions of resistance on the collective level, and the opportunity to begin to develop, adapt and refine individual achievement.

Rebel Voices

Marronage among the new blacks is a subject laded with burning questions and with a long trail of light attached to the feet of the fugitive. Marronage, we know, was a very common recourse and very current in latter days of the colony as it had been earlier. Wish it or not, this approach leads us far away from the idea of a simple malady of the colonial system. We are confronted not with fugitives interested in timid, short-lived escapades, but with true rebels—aggressive, determined, and hostile to slavery. What is more, how could we have not, in all logic, ended up with the indispensable complicities, the secret organizations, and the hidden networks of resistance to slavery?[23]

Definitions of community remain vague. The most fundamental common denominator within political thought discourse concerned with definitions of community is that a community must be more than a collection of individuals living in close proximity to one another. Political thought concerning the concept of community is primarily concerned with order, justice and development. For the most part, the conceptualization of those experiences in regards to Black people and Black communities has been problematic in Western political thought. That is in part because Western political thought has been primarily concerned with competition within and among communities and the development of definitions of community has been an essential part of those competitions.

What we need to identify, at this juncture, is a few major characteristics of community beyond proximity. The first major component is commonly referred to as that of order and/or justice. All arguments arising under these two concepts are circumscribed under the experience of constraint.[24] Arguments of justice and arguments of order are arguments over which concepts, rules, traditions, etc., should constrain individual members and the collective. The second major component is commonly referred to as "development." One critical experience of development is that of transcendence. The ability to transcend environment, and constraints developed within an environment, is essential to the existence of the community and individuals. Much like achievement and resistance, the ability to constrain and the ability to transcend and the way in which this is facilitated, defines not only community in general but particular communities—one from the other.

Theoretically and ideologically, Maroon communities in Haiti, the United States and elsewhere throughout the Diaspora developed as sovereign entities, transcending European constraints. This is somewhat of a romantic notion. In reality, the existence and development of Maroon communities were much more complex. The one thing we can say for certain in this area is that Maroon communities developed the potential for sovereignty. Some approached that potential much more than others. Within these communities developed essential common principles and values that help to inform us about the nature and development of Black political morality. These essential principles and values were initially articulated through common experiences. These essential experiences include inclusiveness, plurality, self-determination and the development of a unique African-centered political morality that, more often than not, came into conflict with Euro-centric understandings of morality.

Myriad Black experiences and institutions developed from Maroon communities, most notably the Haitian revolution and the nation of Haiti. These communities also developed a unique voice, a voice that spoke to Blacks about what it meant to be Black and human. As they became successful in resistance, they converted resistance into achievement by aggregating Blackness. As they found resource in Blackness and the aggregation of Blackness, they stand as the first communities to institutionalize Black identity beyond the level of family.

The first level of achievement is aggregation of individuals with the will, intelligence, skill and good fortune to gain their freedom. Campbell informs us that marronage was well established in Hispaniola, the first European colony in the Americas, as early as 1503, two years after the start of the slave trade in the Caribbean. Campbell's claim is that "by the middle of the 16th century runaways outnumbered Hispaniola's white male population seven to one."[25] This produced communities remarkably dynamic in nature.

Maroon communities, at least initially, needed to be both inclusive and to closely scrutinize potential members. Most sources support this early duality.[26] The inclusiveness existed for most Maroon communities regardless of African cultural group, and sometimes existed regardless of race.[27] Inclusiveness precipitated an aggregation of ideas, philosophies, leaders, skills, etc.

This second level of achievement Fouchard understood in the context of spiritual pluralism:

> Thus it appears that the Voodoo chants reflect more the recognition of "loas" of all the "nations" populating Saint-Domingue, more an affirmation of the plurality of inputs to the formation of Voodoo itself than an ethnic distribution.[28]

The necessity of pluralism produced remarkable individuals who were able to lead diverse cultural and ethnic groups under the most adverse conditions. Women as well as men rose to leadership positions within Maroon communities, although men predominated leadership roles. What these men and women had in common is that they were able to develop leadership styles that addressed the diverse concerns of their communities at the level of existence. All commentaries on Maroon communities stress the importance of African spirituality as part of the Maroon experience. Campbell connects that importance to community leadership:

> Indeed maroon leaders were expected to be imbued with transcendental knowledge, which could be used for the benefit of the community as a whole. Resistance and African religions are clearly linked in both slave rebellions (for instance in Haiti) and maroon societies. Regardless of ethnicity, Africans would invariably invoke the right loas (spirit) before going to war.[29]

These expectations appear phenomenal given the diversity of most Maroon communities. That these leaders were able to find common territory upon which to found and develop these communities is no small achievement. The constant upon which these leaders based their leadership was self-determination:

> Every observer, and Toussaint himself, thought that the labourers were following him because of his past services and his unquestioned superiority. This insurrection proved that they were following him because he represented that complete emancipation from their former degradation which was their chief goal. As soon as he was no longer going to this end, they were ready to throw him over.[30]

Self-determination provided the strongest common bond connecting the community across its various elements within the environs in which Maroons flourished. This was understandable. What this means in the context of Black political morality is that these communities, the first sovereign Black communities in the new world constituted through some element of self-selection, initially were communities predominantly organized around the experience of resistance.

However, it was a different type of resistance than that experienced within the communities of bonded Black people. Unlike Africans who daily resisted the dehumanization of slavery, Maroon resistance was the resistance of one sovereign collective against another. For Blacks within Maroon communities, the question became less of a moral one and more a question of practical strength. Their resistance to the environment depended exactly upon their ability to control their environment. This attempt to control centered their resistive activities:

> They burned San Domingo flat so that at the end of the war it was a charred desert. Why do you burn everything? Asked a French officer of a prisoner. We have a right to burn what we cultivate because a man has a right to dispose of his own labour was the reply of this unknown anarchist.[31]

Just as important was the fact that Maroon communities did not have to totally focus on resistance. Maroon communities afforded individuals and the collective leisure from constant resistance to develop a fundamental level of achieve-ment. They raised cattle, cared for farms, raided plantations for both supplies and human beings and they aggregated territory. Not of least importance is the fact that building a community of diversified tasks and interests allowed the Maroons to aggregate time and leisure to develop experiences of excellence in specialized tasks such as military prowess, political leadership and spiritual leadership.

The development of Maroon communities presents us with some interesting phenomena. A more complete and more distinctly defined individual emerges with-in the Maroon community than on the plantation or even on the flight from plan-tation. We move from the healer/spiritual advisor, such as Douglass found in the slave Sandy Jenkins, to more broadly focused leaders such as Nanny, Mackandal or Boukman. Maroon leadership needed to be not only accomplished in military/spiritual leadership, they also had to, no doubt, develop and administer the community on a daily, nonmilitary basis, or at least recognize this excellence in oth-ers to the degree that it could be developed and utilized for the good of the community.

Successful Maroon communities and their leaders faced even tougher chal-lenges when they became large enough, strong enough, to acquire for themselves the status of autonomous, sometimes sovereign entities. More often than not, they achieved this status through successful conflict with European colonial gov-ernments. Development produced not only privilege but also competition with larg-er and more established political entities that most often had more resources in the sense of institutions, technology and history.

It is in the midst of this conflict that Maroon communities faced a critical ques-tion concerning the relationship between achievement and resistance. In general terms it is a question of how we order the world in relation to those stronger than us and those weaker than us, in particular it was a question of Maroons ordering the world between themselves, the colonial power and their fellow Africans still held in bondage. Obviously, this was an extremely complicated question, one fur-ther complicated by the fact that most individuals of Maroon communities had recently endured the atrocities of slavery and most likely had family still enslaved. The answer to this question contributes much in our attempt to reconstruct the development of Black political morality within the Diaspora, since it represents one of the early significant developments of Black political morality in the Western Hemisphere.

Very early in their development, Maroon communities were inclusive, accept-ing of most, if not all, genuine fugitives from bondage. (We have no reason to believe otherwise; in fact, all available data suggests this was the case.) They made raids upon plantations as a way of further recruiting and building the Maroon com-munity. Most communities began as predominantly male communities, but as they expanded, the ratio of males to females became more normative and eventually women and children outnumbered men.[32] In many ways, without survey data, it appears that most Maroon communities at least initially continued to engage in a conflict with slavery. Maroon communities formulated and implemented both small- and large-scale plans to free other slaves. In fact, Toussaint formulated and Dessalines attempted to implement a dynamic plan to end slavery as a system.

If the ultimate function of the Maroon community was to develop self-determination to the extent of sovereignty, then the development of most Maroon communities was aborted, constrained, or retarded (or the Haitian revolution was in many ways a child prodigy). Just as the planter regime offered benefits to individual enslaved Africans for capturing, killing or informing upon Maroons, the same regime often enlisted the aid of Maroon communities to capture Africans attempting to escape bondage. Maroon communities even turned on other Maroon communities at the demand of the colonial power. Campbell records an instance of a captured Maroon leader escaping "execution by offering to lead expeditions against his former colleagues."[33] In fact each of these acts described were at times experiences of the force Toussaint and Dessalines eventually led to emancipate the people of Haiti.

No matter how we conceptualize the argument concerning this aspect of Maroon existence, what we must eventually come back to is the issue of control versus equality. It is obviously an extremely difficult question because Maroon achievement had fundamentally changed the nature of the community. It would have been very difficult for these communities to go back to pre-marronage slavery, but it was also equally difficult for them to return to the early stages of community development when they were small and mobile enough to wage effective guerilla warfare. Success, which increased their numbers and normalized the ratio of men to women to children, took away from the initial mobility of Maroon communities and consequently exposed them to more extensive and aggressive colonial military power. Like most who gain significant control over themselves and within their environment, Maroons were not willing to totally give up that control. Their alternative was to give up external control and attempt to retain internal control.

Internal control is self-control. External control is exploitation to the degree that it requires us to restrain, constrain and limit that which is beyond ourselves. While each of these experiences is interesting within itself, it is really the relationship between the two that is most interesting and revealing. The relationship is interesting because it has always been believed in Western philosophy that the two experiences were co-dependent—individuals who exerted control over others were thought to be able to do so exactly because they exerted adequate control over themselves. The relationship is revealing because the experience of Black people during the early stages of the Diaspora was significantly different. The primary difference is that Black people observed early that the more Anglo Americans controlled, the more they sought to control, and the more they exhibited a lack of self-control. In fact, one could argue that this lack of self-control appeared to develop at an inverse rate to the extent to which one controlled others and the environment. In fact, as we have seen in the previous section, that is precisely what those held in bondage argued concerning plantation owners and managers. Obviously, one could, and many do, extend this argument to the collective level—group, culture, society, and nation.

How each Maroon community answered this question of internal versus external control contributes to the Black understanding of excellence and moral virtue. In giving up their ability to control the environment—most notably, their competition with other sovereign entities—these communities believed they could preserve their internal self-control. Instead they found themselves forced once again into a one-dimensional existence; moved entirely out of the realm of achievement, they were constrained by the need to continually engage in resistive activities similar to slave communities.

Ultimately, many communities were willing to hand over to the European colonial powers their own and other Black peoples' ability to internally control themselves, simply to maintain a semblance of achievement. In essence, what these communities affected was the narrowing of their own and other Black peoples' development. They found themselves a simple niche performing tasks for the colonial powers, in essence becoming a police force against other Black communities and themselves.

After generations, some of these "Maroon" communities had become so one-dimensional that they perceived mercenary activities as the only virtuous form of life.[34] Such one-dimensionality was obviously a severe limit on development and the ability to adapt and survive. Absent a broad-based perspective, it is questionable whether they could ever develop a political morality conducive to self-discipline, much less maintain the needed balance between exploitation of the environment and equality within the environment. Within such communities flourished an understanding of excellence based predominantly on power. In fact, the particular Maroon community mentioned above ended up being moved to Freetown Harbor, Sierra Leone, at the expense of the British and Canadian governments, "where upon disembarking they assisted in quelling the insurrection of the black Loyalists who had previously emigrated from Nova Scotia."[35]

The Haitian revolution, initiated by Maroons, presents us with an alternative to Maroon communities who chose to cooperate with colonial regimes. There are many aspects of the Haitian revolution that are revealing. C.L.R. James reconstructs the revolutionists as relentless, spirited, and in many ways single-minded in pursuit of their ultimate goal—self-determination. However, his reconstruction of most of the Maroon leaders is somewhat different:

> The leaders of a revolution are usually those who have been able to profit by the cultural advantages of the system they are attacking and the San Domingo revolution was no exception to this rule.[36]

James' reconstruction hints at the possible conflict between the rank-and-file Maroons bent on totally dismantling the slave system and constructing a free Black society, and many of their leaders whose concerns were more of replacing White elitism with Black elitism, taking over and administering the colonial structure, and becoming an integral part of France, the colonizing power.

In fact, James, in what functions as an apology for the great Black general Toussaint, argues that Toussaint's attachment to French culture, his desire to gain respect in the minds of his French counterparts, especially Napoleon, severed him from the very community that he led. James' argument is that while Toussaint believed the slaves were following him for his excellence, they were actually focused on the goal of liberation and were willing to throw the general over when he no longer promised them an avenue to their goal.[37]

James' conclusion, while fundamentally correct, is in some ways incomplete. It was not simply that the Black masses threw over Toussaint's excellence to achieve their goal. In fact, it would be more accurate to conclude that they went beyond Toussaint's understanding of excellence. Achievement for these revolutionaries began with the dismantling of the slave system and all that supported the system. At the end, the revolutionary army was willing to burn everything on the island to prevent the reinstitution of slavery.[38]

One Haitian leader stands apart from the others, even Toussaint, and not necessarily due to his ability to lead the Blacks of Haiti to independence. Jean Jacques Dessalines was of opposite temperament to the leader to whom he (until the very last moment) exhibited so much loyalty and compassion. In many ways, both practical and theoretical, he is indistinguishable from the masses. Uneducated, intensely emotional and unpredictable, given Western European standards, Dessalines was not formally educated and, unlike Toussaint, appears to have had no lasting desire to become educated in the European tradition. He fought with his troops in the midst of the battle, earning respect for his prowess in action. Exhorting, criticizing, praising, he was a charismatic leader who severely detested slavery and slave owners:

> Take courage, I tell you, take courage. The French will not be able to remain long in San Domingo. They will do well at first, but soon they will fall ill and die like flies. Listen! If Dessalines surrenders to them a hundred times he will deceive them a hundred times. I

repeat, take courage, and you will see that when the French are few we shall harass them, we shall beat them, we shall burn the harvests and retire to the mountains. They will not be able to guard the country and will have to leave. Then I shall make you *independent*. There will be no more whites among us." [39]

Dessalines' short speech, which James reconstructs as an exhortation to battle, is much more; it is nothing less than a justification for his style of leadership and a request for the revolutionary army to have faith in his leadership style—his strong will, which provided the foundation for his pursuit of excellence.

James' reconstruction of Dessalines as a leader is never quite favorable. Despite Dessalines' success in finally bringing independence to the Black masses, James' depiction of his character, his faculties, is overly critical and often brutal. To James, Dessalines is a "one-sided genius."[40] He argues that Dessalines' marriage to a cultured Black women, if it had been allowed more time, might have reigned in his wildness.[41] The ultimate condemnation comes in the appendix when James calls Dessalines a "barbarian."[42]

I do not believe that James' condemnation comes because it is Dessalines who suggests to the French that Toussaint be removed from the island. On the contrary, James sees Toussaint's removal as necessary for Haitian Independence. Toussaint's problem goes beyond the lack of communication between him and his troops. The more essential problem is his lack of emotional identification with the Black masses of Haiti. In fact, one can see between the lines of James' work that Toussaint's acculturation reigns in his emotions *too* much. Toussaint's acculturation was, after all, French, and too late did the great Black general realize his primary enemy as France. James constructs this argument to defend Dessalines' abandonment of his beloved commander.

The analytical turning point of *The Black Jacobins* comes in James' understanding, or lack thereof, concerning Dessalines' experience of excellence. At issue in James' work, the reason he is ambivalent concerning Toussaint and Dessalines, is indeed two distinct understandings of excellence, that most essential tool of virtue. For James, the tragedy of Toussaint is that the general has the foundation to develop what James understands as a broad intellectual understanding of life. In essence, James perceives Toussaint as a philosopher-ruler who could have developed a broad-based diverse society capable of competing with modern European nations. Yet, Toussaint fails to bring independence to the Black masses of Haiti.

Dessalines, however, is another matter for James. He is the barbarian. This label is applicable to Dessalines, for James, on many levels. James' early pronunciation that leaders of revolutions "are usually those who have been able to profit by the cultural advantages of the system they are attacking" does not apply to Dessalines.[43] In fact the only "advantage" that the early "barbarians" who were most responsible for conceiving and initiating the Haitian revolution took from the French colo-

nial regime was their freedom. Neither the one-handed Mackandal nor his successor, Boukman, the priest, took any "cultural advantage" from the colonial regime.[44]
The last "barbarian" to ascend to leadership of the revolution, Dessalines, was in
the worst position to take advantage of the "cultural advantages" of the colonial
regime. Dessalines was the slave of a Black man. That individual was most likely
the descendant of slaves. By James' own description, the individual who held
Dessalines in bondage had not spared the use of the whip and did not inspire in
Dessalines the loyalty that Toussaint exhibited in saving his mistress and her
family during the early stages of the revolution.[45] In fact, all reports indicate
Dessalines killed his master before leaving the plantation during the early stages
of the revolt. Yet, Dessalines is the one who leads the Black masses in Haiti to
independence.

The truth is that James has extreme difficultly understanding and articulating
the excellence of Dessalines. For James, Dessalines' virtue is vague, allusive, except
on the basest level. That which is recognizable in Dessalines is his love of equality, his loyalty, his love of freedom and his endurance and intensity, his will:

> Unfortunate Martiniquans, I am not able to fly to your assistance and break your chains.
> Alas, an invincible obstacle separates us . . . but perhaps a spark from the fire which we have
> kindled will spring forth in your soul.[46]

Two years after independence, in 1806, Dessalines is assassinated, partially
because he is looking for a way to redistribute land to the Black masses. This
would have entailed some confiscation of land from mulatto hands. The mulattos
had inherited the land from their French fathers when the latter fled the island in
light of the revolutionary victory:

> The sons of the colonists have taken advantage of my poor blacks. Be on your guard,
> Negroes and mulattoes, we have all fought against the whites; the properties which we have
> conquered by the spilling of our blood belong to us all; I intend that they be divided with
> equity.[47]

Even with the possibility of redistribution, Dessalines was after bringing
Haitians together regardless of African or European ancestry. Nicholls, in his short
passage on "Dessalines and Black Liberation," sums up, perhaps, the true excellence
of Dessalines and the Black masses:

> The first constitution of Haiti proclaimed that all Haitians no matter what their shade of
> skin were to be called "black"; this included even those German and Polish groups in Saint
> Domingue who had fought with the liberation movement and had become citizens. Perhaps
> this is the first time that the term "black" has been used in an ideological sense.[48]

Even Nicholls' excellent analysis slightly misses the mark. For Dessalines and
his "poor Blacks," Blackness entailed an experience, in essence a philosophy of exis-

tence, an alternative philosophy to that produced and maintained by Western Europe. The problem for Dessalines and the Black masses of Haiti is that no commentator on either Dessalines or the Haitian revolution has been able to articulate the parameters of that philosophy. But within the Black Diaspora, this failure is widespread. Most commentators on the new Blacks have failed to adequately understand this sense of excellence, much less define its parameters. This has not simply been a failure of commentators:

> Much in Negro life remains a mystery; perhaps the zoot suit conceals profound political meaning; perhaps the symmetrical frenzy of the Lindy Hop conceals clues to great potential power—if only Negro leaders would solve this riddle.[49]

Unchained Voices: Free Black Communities

> I found the colored people much more spirited than I had supposed they would be. I found among them a determination to protect each other form the blood-thirsty kidnapper, at all hazards. Soon after my arrival, I was told of a circumstance which illustrated their spirit. A colored man and a fugitive slave were on unfriendly terms. The former was heard to threaten the latter with informing his master of his whereabouts. Straightway a meeting was called among the colored people, under the stereotyped notice, "Business of importance!" The betrayer was invited to attend. The people came at the appointed hour, and organized the meeting by appointing a very religious old gentlemen as president, who, I believe, made a prayer, after which he addressed the meeting as follows: "Friends, we have got him here, and I would recommend that you young men just take him outside the door, and kill him!" With this a number of them bolted at him; but they were intercepted by some more timid than themselves, and the betrayer escaped their vengeance, and has not been seen in New Bedford since. There have been no more such threats, and should there be hereafter, I doubt not that death would be the consequence.[50]

Black people in states that declared slavery illegal found themselves in an environment that was remarkably different from the environment of Blacks still held in bondage or that of Blacks within Maroon communities. It is within Black communities in free Northern and Western states that Black people initially experience and begin to develop the foundation of double consciousness as a functional political morality. Also within these communities, the political conflict that eventually develops into political stasis begins to develop. That political conflict is a direct effect of the double consciousness and has a significant influence upon Black political development.

Free Black people, unlike Black people still held in bondage, did not need to sustain a constant struggle against an outside community, at least not to develop and maintain the fundamental institutions of humanity—individuality and family. These communities were able to orient these fundamental institutions more toward the experience of achievement even though other immediate dangers, such as violent Anglo American riots, always loomed nearby. Discourses and institutions concerned with the development of the individual and family developed within free Black communities relatively unconstrained by any outside source. Like Maroon communities, emerging free Black communities in the North continued to struggle against at least portions of communities with better resources and organization than themselves. However, the daily struggle did not hold the possibility of constant military threat from a sovereign political entity. Overall, the immediate concern, for free Black communities, is less one of daily existence and resistance and one more concerned with the quality of existence and achievement.

Free Blacks communities still faced the same fundamental challenge as their enslaved and outlawed counterparts—that of proving their humanity. That challenge came from Anglo American communities more in the context of individual and collective superiority versus inferiority. However, leisure (relative to their enslaved and Maroon counterparts) afforded free Blacks the choice to gauge the essentialness of these challenges in relation to their individual and aggregate existence and desire for achievement:

> Although some free Blacks could always be found among the slave insurrectionists and conspirators, the majority of leading free Black abolitionists let considerations of property and civic gentility sway them toward reform. Thus, long after free Black workers began to sour on the new country, the free Black middle class remained enchanted by the possibility of achieving equality in America. Black men and women of influence rallied their communities to the defense of Philadelphia and New York during the war of 1812.[51]

In short, Black people in the North, especially an emerging Black elite, were free to enjoy a significant portion of their humanity—individual self-determination, family, community, and achievement. Indeed they were able to take for granted development and maintenance of these most fundamental human institutions.

Initially, free Blacks outside of the South only perceived particular portions of the Anglo American community as an immediate existential threat. As a consequence, the struggle over dehumanization, Black humanity, developed more within the constraints of philosophical discourse as opposed to the aggregation of daily experiences that drove the development of resistance of Blacks still held in bondage. Such struggles in modern Western societies are typically controlled by elites—limited in many ways to those with sufficient leisure and institutional training. In particular, the heightened philosophical level also subjected the conflict to the development of universal understandings between Blacks and Anglo Americans. In the early stages of development, pursuit of humanity as a philosophical endeavor put free Black Northern communities at a disadvantage and severely retarded the development of a political morality based upon the Black experience. There are very few universal experiences between a collective who must prove its membership in the human species and a collective who not only takes its membership for granted but also experiences its culture as the epitome of humanity. In absence of those universals, the discourse developed along the lines of Anglo American cultural superiority.

Early in the history of Black America, most free Blacks adopted the Anglo American Christian experience as a significant foundation for Black political morality. The reasons for adopting this experience were many. First and foremost was the linkage between humanness and the major tenets of Christianity. Of essential importance to Blacks were that these tenets developed out of a historical experience (Jewish biblical history articulated in the First Testament of the Bible) very similar to the Black experience.[52] This was paralleled by a general belief that when Blacks proved their Christian worthiness, inclusiveness into the American experience would be forthcoming. Black people also perceived Christianity as the most viable method of moderating and effecting Anglo American behavior.

Free Blacks not only patronized Anglo American institutions (most of which were centered around the Anglo American Christian experience) but began to develop a variety of institutions ranging from fraternal orders to separate Black churches. These institutions were culturally unique because that which tied them together was their participation in a unique discourse centered in the Black community and the Black psyche. Still, essential principles and values that were the base of these institutions were adapted from the Anglo American Christian experience, as understood by free Blacks.

This assessment of the value of the Anglo American Christian experience, especially in the significance it played upon Northern Anglo Americans, was astute and centered around a particular phenomenon that arose in 17th-century New England:

> The American jeremiad arose as a form of ritualistic complaint and self-reproach because of the apparent failure of Puritan society to fulfill its task of self-perfection and world redemption. Jeremiads, a speech pattern named after the plaintive biblical prophet Jeremiah, were ringing from New England pulpits with swelling ferocity by 1650. These jeremiads deplored a long list of perceived social ills, denounced the people for their sins and misconduct, and warned of worse tribulations and divine punishments to come if they did not quickly repent and observe their social covenant . . . the complete rhetorical ritual, for Berocovitch, is comprised of three parts: citing of the promise, lamentation of present declension, and a prophecy of the promise's imminent fulfillment.[53]

The American jeremiad exhibited two other essential components: "unshakable optimism" and the Puritan belief in America as a chosen land and themselves as a chosen people.[54] This experience is best articulated in John Winthrop's treatise, *A Model of Christian Charity*:

> For we must consider that we shall be as a city upon a hill. The eyes of all people are upon us. So that if we shall deal falsely with our God in this work we have undertaken, and so cause Him to withdraw His present help from us, we shall be made a story and a by-word through the world. We shall open the mouths of enemies to speak evil of the ways of God, and all professors for God's sake. We shall shame the faces of many of God's worthy servants, and cause their prayers to be turned into curses upon us till we be consumed out of the good land whither we are going.[55]

Howard-Pitney, reconstructing the work of Bercovitch, concludes that the American jeremiad became the core of Anglo American national culture, expanded to include all North American Protestants by the early 18th century, and by the 19th century was the foundation for the secular mission of spreading the blessings of democracy and free enterprise throughout the world.[56]

Howard-Pitney's conclusion that concerns us at the moment is that the "American jeremiad has been frequently adapted and used for the purposes of Afro-American protest and propaganda."[57] Charles Henry echoes Howard-Pitney, concluding that the Afro American jeremiad evolved out of the Anglo American jeremiad as an explanation for the collective suffering of Black people.[58]

For both, the Black jeremiad developed around the question of abolition of slavery and "had its deepest roots in the Northern black community."[59] The Black jeremiad held to Winthrop's central tenets that Americans were a chosen people and America a chosen land. Free Blacks integrated the "unshakable optimism" into their discourse concerning the question of slavery. And when Anglo Americans showed any hesitancy in ending slavery, they denounced the American experience as being false to its mission:

> No people in this world make louder pretensions to "liberty, equality, and the rights of man," than the people of the South! And yet, strange as it may appear, there is no spot in the United States where oppression reigns with such unlimited sway! It is here we may see human nature sunk to the lowest state of degradation; and human misery exalted to a height, which if transcended, would be beyond human endurance.[60]

Although free Blacks were astute in their understanding of the degree to which the American jeremiad influenced Anglo American thought, they also overestimated its influence in connection to ending slavery and other essential questions of dehumanization. The most fundamental error made by many free Blacks was in simply adopting by faith the argument that America was a chosen land and Americans were a chosen people destined for moral perfection. This belief in Anglo American progress toward perfection provided the foundation for the adoption of moral suasion as the primary method of opposing the institution of slavery. Obviously, as adopted by Anglo American Christians, it fit well with this understanding of progress toward perfection by Anglo American Protestants. It also fit well into the goals of free Blacks and their desire to be accepted as full-fledged Americans by their Northern Anglo American neighbors.

Moral suasion advocated ending slavery by persuading advocates of slave owning that the ownership of other human beings was morally reprehensible, or evil. Moral suasion opposed the use of coercion and/or violence. The paradigm allowed Northern Anglo Americans and free Blacks who championed the experience two positives: adherents remained in a sense "unsoiled" by slavery and in this sense continuing their progression toward perfection; and also, through rhetorical spiritualism, they were able to lift up the less fortunate in the South, slave owners and slaves alike, assisting them onto the path toward perfection.

In the adoption of Christianity, the American jeremiad and moral suasion by free Blacks, much rested upon a leap of faith. That leap of faith lay in the myth of Anglo American progress toward moral/spiritual perfection. Free Blacks should have found reason to pause when Puritans themselves were never able to achieve this perfection. Eventually, moral suasion gave way to more active opposition to slavery, even among a significant portion of Anglo American abolitionists. In *Black Movements in America*, Cedric Robinson argues that "abolitionism manifested itself in three phases: the elitist phase, militant populist phase and the revolutionary phase."[61] The elitist phase, roughly the first 50 years after the American Revolution, finds abolition developing within urban centers among mostly moderate leaders and fueled by the argument of "moral (Christian) suasion rather than by force or insurrection."[62] In the 1830s, the movement began to shift toward a more radical social element grounded in rural areas. The ideology also shifted to a more radical Christianity, which in some instances advocated "precipitous" action such as going into slave states and encouraging slaves to escape.[63] Eventually the frustration over the conflict produces John Brown's aborted revolution.

What the frustration of the Anglo American Christian analysis of slavery produced was in fact a microcosm of one of the historical symptoms of the European Christian experience. The Christian experience helped to develop deep divides in Europe. The Protestant movement, despite its benefits, exacerbated those divisions. The divisions continued to develop despite European emigration. In fact, the First Amendment to the United States Constitution, which separates church and state, is evidence of exactly how divisive the political and economic elite of the newly formed country believed questions of Christianity were. Even though the American jeremiad tended to unify Americans against outside threats, it is divisive among Americans themselves. Some of the initial evidence of that divisiveness appears at this early stage, not simply between Anglo American abolitionists and Anglo American slave owners but among Anglo American abolitionists themselves. The divides were not superficial. In fact, these divisions created a political stasis over both the subject and object of slavery (Black Americans) that is written into the U.S. Constitution and burned into American political morality and the American psyche.

Not surprisingly, as the free Black population adopted the Christian experience of the Northern Anglo American population as a foundation of political thought, they could not constrain its propensity toward producing divisions within a particular collective. The divisiveness that was fueled by the myth of Anglo American progress toward perfection infused itself deeper into Black political morality because of a variety of factors. The first two factors have to do with the Black experience. First, the American jeremiad developed out of a particular European experience that covered more than five centuries of development, and free Blacks had very little access to the depth, width or breadth of this development. In short, they had no way of gauging the accuracy of the interpretation or goals of that experience. Second, one reason why Blacks had very little access to the Anglo American political/moral experience is because they had developed their own unique experience for more than two hundred years. That Black experience, in many ways directly and necessarily, opposed the myth of Anglo American perfection. This is especially true in the South, were the majority of Blacks, nearly a ten-to-one majority in relation to free Blacks in Northern and Western states, had developed a spiritual tradition markedly different than that adopted from the American jeremiad.

As free Blacks became increasingly frustrated with American willingness to compromise their safety and well-being, as more Blacks escaped the South and began to fulfill essential functions in the development of Black political morality, a divide with significant consequences began to develop within Black political morality. To fully understand that divide we must return to the work of Frederick Douglass.

Despite the phases of abolitionism, the ideology of moral suasion remained dominant up until the eve of the Civil War. Frederick Douglass, the most popular Black proponent of moral suasion, broke with William Lloyd Garrison, the most popular Anglo American proponent of moral suasion in 1849.[64] Garrison's activities continued to be supported and funded by leading Black businessmen, professionals, clergy and congregations up to the eve of the Civil War.[65]

The fact is, the split between Douglass and the moral-suasion group was a fundamental split and a split that was deemed necessary for Douglass exactly because moral suasion and the context out of which it came had forced a political stasis upon the Black community. While all free Blacks may have been able to recognize the stasis, Douglass is rare among the Black elite in his reassessment of fundamental principles and values. The essential argument that drives this section's analysis is as follows: Douglass is able to achieve that which many free Blacks were unable or unwilling to achieve exactly because he came from a different political and moral context than most free Blacks. Douglass is one of the first Black thinkers/leaders to exhibit within his work the tension between two consciousnesses. This should not be surprising, since Douglass' work offers an essential foundation for Du Bois' arguments in *Souls of Black Folk*.[66]

Howard-Pitney argues that Douglass was one of the essential figures in developing the Black jeremiad. Howard-Pitney's argument is based almost solely upon a cursory examination of the content of Douglass' speeches. Such an argument would hold well for Douglass during his adherence to moral suasion; but after his split with Garrison, it is hard to place Douglass within the tradition because of his reliance upon his experiences during his bondage and his resistance to that bondage, which Douglass draws upon to transcend the concept of moral suasion.

Earlier during this inquiry, the conclusion was held that Douglass and other newly freed Blacks would have an increased inclination toward the pursuit of equality through nonviolent means because of the heightened spiritualism required for resistance to oppression. It is that heightened spiritualism that initially brings Douglass into the moral-suasion camp. Douglass was, after all, an ex-slave attempting to establish for himself not just a new life, but a new identity of which violence—even violence as a last resort to defend oneself or resist oppression—was part of a former life that he and most other ex-slaves wanted to commit to memory. For such individuals, the American jeremiad offered a welcome alternative, and the belief in America as a chosen land and Americans as a chosen people in many ways was redemptive.

What Douglass and other ex-slaves found in light of this new life, free of the need of physical resistance, was that slave owners constantly sought to reconstruct both their enslavement and their dehumanization. Douglass and a large portion of the Black community became disillusioned by the fact that non-slave-owning Americans constantly compromised Black freedom and humanity for political and economic gain. It appears that for Douglass, as for many other Black people in the United States, the passage of the Fugitive Slave Act was the culmination of this disillusionment and the end of the context in which they could fully subscribe to the American jeremiad. Literally for Douglass and other Blacks, the United States was no longer a promised land, and Americans themselves represented opportunists who posed a constant threat to both Black freedom and Black humanity.

Douglass' disillusionment represents a fundamental reassessment of the environment. Given that fundamental reassessment, Douglass and many other free Blacks perceived the United States as a hostile environment. Such a radical shift in perception of one's environment necessitates a shift in political morality.

Douglass and many Black people in the North, including the Black elite, began to stress Black resistance instead of Black achievement. That stress is the foundation for a Black political morality based upon the Black historical experience. Absent the myth of Anglo American progress toward Christian perfection, Douglass and many Blacks had nowhere to turn except toward an in-depth analysis of their own experience.

Bernard Boxill devotes significant energy inquiring into the possibility of Douglass' resistive experiences and the foundation they provide for the development of a unique Black political morality after his split from the camp of moral suasion. Boxill's argument rests upon the assumption that Douglass retained two specific and distinct goals in turning from moral suasion. Those two goals were first, to free slaves, and second, to reform slave owners and other Anglo Americans.[67] Boxill concludes that Douglass transcends moral suasion because it lacks the power to achieve either of the two goals. Douglass concludes that only a more complete form of resistance (which may necessarily include violent, physical action) held the potential power necessary to achieve these goals.

It is Douglass' conception of power, and Boxill's reconstruction of how this conception developed out of the ex-slave abolitionist's pre-freedom experiences that is essential to our inquiry. Boxill reconstructs the following argument based upon Douglass' fight with a slave breaker named Edward Covey, which appears in three of Douglass' autobiographical works, *Narrative of the Life of Frederick Douglass: An American Slave*, *My Bondage and My Freedom*, and *The Life and Times of Frederick Douglass*.

Boxill argues that Douglass develops a "general and uncompromising claim that human nature *cannot* honor a person without power or force."[68] This meant that one must be willing to die to protect oneself and indeed has an absolute right/duty to protect oneself from physical abuse that attempted to render one into a position so degraded that they would never be able to recover their humanity.[69] According to Boxill, experience taught Douglass that pity would not turn the heart of the slave owner nor influence others standing by and watching to help; but when a slave was subjected to these conditions, they must fight. In fact, slavery had hardened the hearts of slave owners and corrupted the rest of America so thoroughly that neither retained the capacity to act on emotions such as pity for Blacks held in bondage.[70] The final point that Boxill reconstructs is that Douglass believed that Blacks should resist the will of those oppressing them by any means necessary because resistance was not only essential in redeeming Black humanity, but placed upon the slave owners' doors the only emotion upon which they would be willing to act—fear.

From his analysis of these experiences as presented in the three autobiographies, Boxill claims that Douglass developed a unique understanding of power:

If this is true to Douglass' meaning his remarks on power and its relation to honor and dignity bear a second interpretation. Power is not simply a demonstrated willingness to stand up for the principles of morality. It is also a capacity to arouse the fear of others. On this account Douglass would be an advocate of Black Power, though not perhaps in the manner of his great contemporary Martin Delany. For Delany, Black Power was necessary for blacks to avoid white oppression. For Douglass, Black Power was also necessary for blacks and whites to have a sense of morality.[71]

While Boxill's work is excellent, there is a moment of hesitation:

> We should therefore remember that Douglass' experience with resistance was fortunate, though not altogether unprecedented or unique. Resistance was generally a very dangerous business. And this suggests a further difficulty. If continuous or unpredictable physical mistreatment can distract a man from thoughts of his moral status, degrade him, and make him incapable of acting morally, then surely the fear of being suddenly cut off can have the same result, and perhaps even more effectively. But in that case resistance seems a bad bargain. Indeed it seems to be a way of jumping from the frying pan into the fire.[72]

Boxill's attempt to resolve this moment of hesitation proves inadequate:

> Douglass seems to have anticipated this difficulty. He had, he said, "reached the point at which he was not afraid to die." Although life was precious to him, and he did not wish his death, since he was not afraid to die, he was not agitated and distracted by the thought that he could be killed because of his resistance. It was a settled point for him that he would die rather than fail to resist physical abuse. His mind was therefore free to reflect on his equal moral status.[73]

The mistake that Boxill makes is attempting to cast something endemic to all philosophical arguments—necessary leaps of faith—into rational terms. This particular attempt leaves the reader unsatisfied and fails to articulate the strength of Douglass' actions or the depths of a separate Black political morality.

> And far from being intimidated, the civic population met the terror with such courage and firmness as frightened the terrorists. Three blacks were condemned to be burnt alive. A huge crowd stood round while two of them were consumed, uttering horrible cries. But the third, a boy of 19, bound so that he could not see the other two, called to them in the Creole, "You do not know how to die. See how to die." By great effort he twisted his body in his bonds, sat down and, placing his feet in the flames, let them burn without uttering a groan.[74]

The ambivalence that is prevalent in the passage written by Douglass is far from prevalent in the actions of the 19-year-old Haitian rebel. There is for the rebel no speculation concerning his resistance. Much like Douglass, the young rebel appears to have decided that he would not fear death if it came as a consequence of resistance. Yet, if we pick up on Boxill's metaphor, the young rebel appears to have reaffirmed the value of his resistance exactly because it has landed him in the fire.

And if James' reconstruction of the reaction of the French officer present at the execution is correct, then all of the results Boxill argues for concerning Douglass' construction of power are present in this example. Still, this does nothing to achieve the ultimate goal of Douglass and the young rebel. Neither the fear of Covey nor that of the French officer could help Douglass or our young Haitian rebel redeem Black humanity. Men have the capacity to fear animals and indeed are often awestruck by their actions—it in no way inspires them to think of the animal as human. The reason why fear affects Covey to such a degree is because of Covey's value of fear as a moderating tool of behavior.[75] In the case of the Haitian rebel, the courage and leadership he exhibits is honored by the French officer and has a similar moderating effect upon him. Both Douglass and the young rebel went beyond the limits of Black people as understood by their oppressors. In fact, their resistance took them to a point beyond which their oppressors could themselves have journeyed in similar circumstances.

We are at the juncture where reconstructing a political morality becomes difficult. The difficulty is due to the fact that political morality develops through discourse. Douglass' discourse with Covey, like the young rebel's with the French officer, is evidence that their counterparts have experienced the depths of their own understanding of humanity (or lack thereof) through the unexpected actions of these young Black men. An adequate outcome, but for Douglass and the young rebel the bar was set much higher. The real test of one's humanity is internal. There is much to consider before we can argue that Douglass and the young rebel pass their own tests. For both, Black political morality was youthful and the discourse of political morality very dynamic due to this youthfulness. The young rebel can speak to Haitian excellence through the method of his death. He could hear the lack of excellence and in that moment construct and act upon an understanding of excellence. For Douglass, the ambivalence remains because he is never sure he has achieved his understanding of excellence (his resolve not just to fight, but to not be defeated by Covey). He is never sure he has achieved his understanding of excellence exactly because of Covey's actions after the fight:

> It was for a long time a matter of surprise to me why Covey did not immediately have me taken to the constable to the whipping-post, and there regularly whipped for the crime of raising my hand against a white man in defence of myself. And the only explanation I can now think of does not entirely satisfy me . . .[76]

Douglass, remember, is a 16-year-old youth during the time of the fight. Douglass cannot be certain that he has faced the ultimate test of self-determination exactly because there are no repercussions, and in Douglass' world repercussions are always forthcoming for a rebellious slave. To conclude that he has been successful requires a further leap of faith for Douglass.

Sandy Jenkins offers us a solution to Boxill's dilemma. Jenkins recognized what Boxill ignores:

> Sandy's wife was not behind him in kindness—both seemed to esteem it a privilege to suc-
> cor me; for, although I was hated by Covey and by my master, I was loved by the colored
> people, because *they* thought I was hated for my knowledge, and persecuted because I was
> feared. I was the *only* slave *now* in the region who could read and write. . . . My knowledge
> was now the pride of my brother slaves; and no doubt, Sandy felt something of the gener-
> al interest in me on that account.[77]

What Sandy provides is a means for Douglass to focus his resistance. This allows Douglass to take the leap of faith necessary for a more intense and complete form of resistance. Both faith and resistance, obviously, are qualities that Douglass possesses prior to meeting the older slave. In fact, the Black community values Douglass because he possesses these qualities. The community values not only his skill but also his bravery in acquiring that skill and the faith required to attain such a skill during that particular moment in the development of Black history. In other words, it is not the skill alone that holds the possibility of reaffirming Black humanity. Sandy's talk of roots and resistance provides Douglass with direction, focus. The same type of focus that Maroon leaders provided their rank and file by "invoking the right loa (spirit) before going to war."[78] At the time of their meeting, Douglass was wandering, disoriented, hiding, starving and desperate—the thought of complete resistance had not yet been entertained by the young slave. Sandy provides not only the direction but also the context, and with the context, the *spirit* of Douglass' resistance.

Concerning Sandy, Douglass provides us some essential information. Sandy is a slave who is married to a free woman. Douglass found him "an old adviser." Risking both his and his wife's well-being, he takes Douglass home without being solicited, and the older slave and his wife feed and care for Douglass. He counsels the younger man to return to Covey.[79] This counsel is not based upon the expectations of the master, but upon the probability of success of an immediate escape attempt. For Douglass to return to Covey's farm, he must be both self-determinant and extremely brave. To choose to return despite possible consequences provides the younger slave with a portion of dignity he would not have obtained if he had simply starved in the woods and been found in one exhausted state or another by Covey. The self-determination, bravery and dignity which Sandy points Douglass toward is squarely grounded in the Black slave community. Though some may consider it purely conjecture, it is not a stretch to consider, given Douglass' passage concerning the value the community placed upon his knowledge, that Sandy also considered that which was best for the community in this council.

Douglass obviously had complete trust in the older Black man—there is no hes-itation between ascertaining Sandy's identity and revealing himself. Although Douglass tells us, somewhat ambiguously, that he never really allocated to the root the power that Sandy advisesd, he did recognize in Sandy "too deep an insight into human nature, with all his superstition, not to have some respect for his advice." Not only did Douglass respect him, but "and perhaps, too, a slight gleam or shad-ow of his superstition had fallen upon me." It is upon leaving Sandy and his wife, now "quite courageously," that Douglass decides to resist.[80]

Although Boxill's account over the significance that the fight with Covey has later in Douglass' life is extremely plausible, at 16 years of age such complex philo-sophical understanding was most likely not the reason Douglass found himself imbued with the courage to resist Covey upon leaving Sandy. It was much more straightforward. Sandy provided for Douglass the context upon which to take a leap of faith. To Douglass' credit, he seized upon the opportunity and was success-ful in a circumstance where much older, much stronger men may have failed. Still, it must be argued that Douglass' emerging political morality, and his courage to act upon that political morality, emerged within a specific community context and that Douglass, in fighting, surviving and successfully resisting Covey, simply fulfills the very potential that he himself states the Black community has perceived in him.

It is Douglass' leap of faith, centered in the community that he loves, that allows him to resist Covey and later develop an alternative political morality that transcends moral suasion, the Afro American jeremiad, and its Anglo American Christian roots. This is only achieved as a necessity, even for such a tireless war-rior as Douglass. For most free Black communities, development is similar. Development of a political morality based upon the Black experience only tran-scends the Anglo American Christian paradigm after these communities become frustrated with the actions of Anglo Americans and the inability of Anglo American political morality to influence such actions.

This development for many Blacks is not as easy and as straightforward as it is for Douglass. Consider the life of Richard Allen, the founder of the first African American religious order in the United States. Allen, like Douglass, was born a slave in Philadelphia on February 14th—Allen was born in 1760; Douglass in 1817. For Allen, the success and frustration associated with Anglo American Christianity is extremely ambiguous. Most of Allen's family, his mother, father and three sib-lings were sold when he was eight years old.[81] It is this event that spurs Allen's Methodist conversion.[82] Allen's conversion was complete. Allen became such a devout Methodist that he eventually helped to convert his owner, Stuckley Sturgis, who shortly thereafter allowed Allen and his remaining brother to purchase their freedom. Allen was able to purchase his freedom August 27, 1783.[83]

Soon after purchasing his freedom, Allen left the area to "preach across the state of New Jersey." In the winter of 1785–1786, Allen began the mission that would characterize his entire career. As an assistant minister, he was asked to preach to a small group of Black Methodists attending services at St. George's Church in Philadelphia.[84] In 1794, Allen rejected an offer to become minister at St. Thomas African Episcopal Church due to his love of the Methodist faith. However, due to the racism of the predominantly White Methodist congregation, Allen and the few Black Methodists formed the Bethel African Methodist Church in July of the same year.

The problem for Allen and other Blacks is that their experience with the Methodist faith in Philadelphia was ambiguous. As much as it offered redemption, it reminded them of their imposed inferiority. It could do little to curb the racism of their Anglo American Methodist counterparts and ultimately it could not help them achieve full citizenship status in the United States. In fact, it was the source of an initial split between Allen and Absalom Jones, who accepted the position at St. Thomas African Episcopal Church. Allen's congregation did grow steadily from ten at its founding to more than 1,200 by 1813, but that growth failed to change the way Whites looked at Blacks in the Methodist religion, Philadelphia or the United States. More importantly, it gave Blacks no political control over their own lives. It also never was able to make any inroads concerning the question of Black dehumanization.

Still, Anglo American Christianity had already branded itself upon the psyche of free Blacks in the United States. In some distinct ways transcending American political morality became a dormant, but still accessible, aspect of free Black political morality—the double consciousness brewing below the surface. Taking a critical look at the development of Black political morality in the North we can trace a recurring pattern throughout most eras. That pattern begins with confidence in, and the temporary adoption of, Anglo American political morality to achieve optimist goals. When such goals are met with significant Anglo American opposition or nonsupport, a period of political frustration follows; this period itself provides the foundation for the awakening of a more radical political morality founded upon Black experience developed and articulated in opposition to Anglo American society. Dawson in his recent work, *Black Visions*, found this cycle so prevalent that he reconstructs those caught in its influence as adherents to a particular type of ideology, "disillusioned liberals."[85]

The experience of Black emigration from the United States and other areas in the Black Diaspora, and the questions that surround the experience, form an essential part of the development of the third strain of Black political morality. Even though the actual number of Blacks who emigrated is relatively small in comparison to those who remained, the discourse created by the experience informs one of the most complex and intense conflicts erupting within free Black communities. It appears to have elicited more emotion than did the question of slavery. It also appears, from the Black perspective at least, to have elicited more answers that analyzed the problem from the level of existence:

> The years between 1817 and 1840 provide an interesting format for analyzing thought among free blacks regarding colonization, whether to Guiana, Canada, Haiti, Honduras, Demerara, Trinidad, Texas or elsewhere. Their opinions were expressed in many arguments for and against leaving the land of their birth. They utilized to the maximum the press, conventions and mass meetings, correspondence form émigrés, and the public platform and pulpit.[86]

There are three distinct periods of early Black emigration we need to understand: early development of emigration by Blacks as an alternative to racism and oppression (1776–1817), the development of Black opposition to the American Colonization Society[87] (1817–1850), and the reconstruction of Black self-determinant emigration as an initial development of Black Nationalism (1850–1880). The first period is characterized by exploration and emigration being envisioned as predominantly geared toward Black achievement. The second period is characterized by an existential challenge to what was perceived by most free Blacks as an attempt to compel or trick them into leaving the country. Free Blacks met this challenge by constructing a discourse concerned with resisting dehumanization. Resistance to dehumanization also characterizes the third period of emigration. However, the discourse again favored emigration as a form of Black Nationalism in answer to increasing U.S. segregation and oppression.

The truth is, we can analyze Black emigration from a purely rational perspective for centuries and still only scratch the surface. The question of emigration elicited an intensity of emotion from free Blacks that must be understood:

> This scheme had no sooner been propagated, than the old and leading colored men of Philadelphia, Pa., with Richard Allen, James Forten, and others at their head, true to their trust and the cause of their brethren, summoned the colored people together, and then and there, in language and with voices pointed and loud, protested against the scheme as an outrage, having no other object in view, than the benefit of the slave-holding interests of the country, and that as freemen, they would never prove recreant to the cause of their brethren in bondage, by leaving them without hope of redemption from their chains.[88]

> This is an era, however, in our affairs, that we cannot shut our eyes to, and it must appear to the philosopher, the Christian, and the sagacious politician, a period of deep and anxious solicitude as regards the future prospects, hopes and interests of a people little known but as a nuisance—mere laborers in the most menial capacity . . . [89]

What is missing, in the source, depth and intensity of these emotions, is a love of Africa. In the discourse of free Blacks, we see rational arguments concerning the economic and political potential of enterprising Blacks emigrating to Africa or Haiti, we see arguments concerning the Christian potential of missionary work in Africa and Haiti; however, we see neither a love for the land nor respect for the people as a dominant part of the discourse:

> Having been informed that there was a settlement of people of colour at Sierra Leone under the immediate guardianship of civilized power, I have for these many years past felt a lively interest in their behalf, wishing that the inhabitants of the colony might become established in the truth, and thereby be instrumental in its promotion amongst our African brethren.[90]

This sentiment by Paul Cuffe, the most active voice of our first period of Black emigration, is reflective of all three periods. The idea of "evangelizing Africa" was such a widespread theme, developed in the early period and adopted in the second period as part of the American Colonization Society's platform, that it forms one of the major arguments forwarded by Black people against colonization in the second period:

> But, according to their own reports, whom do they select as instruments to spread civilization and Christianity? People not fit to live in America—people who are a disgrace to that country. I pity Africa as much as any man; I want her to be enlightened; but let us send men who are enlightened themselves. If we mean to evangelize Africa, let us at least send Christians there to do the work.[91]

Absent a love for the land of their ancestors, absent a respect for the people, free Blacks envisioned emigration as a question linked solely to their own existence and development. What would best facilitate the existence and development of Blacks within the United States and throughout the world, emigration or remaining within the confines of the United States? Most free Blacks answered the question by fighting emigration, especially as it was posited by the American Colonization Society. However, no matter how they answered the question, we can see the deep divide apparent in Black thought. Even those who chose to emigrate chose to see emigration as a question of "Black sovereignty," as Robinson characterizes Black emigration; they still chose to carry with them the American jeremiad and still unconsciously envisioned America as the chosen land. They envisioned emigration as bringing the American mission to Africa.

This then is the early cultural context from which Black political morality emerges. We can begin to envision at least three strains all exerting influence upon Black political morality within that cultural context. Black culture has never been monolithic, and Black historians have never told the story of the Black experience as if it were monolithic. Despite the differences among our three strains that contribute to the development of Black political morality within the United States, they share one commonality. Each strain, no matter the degree of influence of Anglo American thought upon that strain, began to develop a theoretical construct of Blackness as an identity. Such constructs were complex, and more often than not they were not bound by physical appearance. The Haitian rebels, part of the strain least under the influence of Western thinking, reconstruct an understanding of Blackness that is based on revolution against oppressive power, straining toward political *and* economic equality, and is not bound by physical appearance, in as much as it could accommodate Europeans as Blacks, due to the fact that they fought with the rebels for independence. The same devaluing of race and ethnicity as a significant factor in constructing identity can be seen in each of the three strains.

CHAPTER
THREE

Black Resistance

When they left by they self you could hear a tapping, tapping, tapping all day and all night. And they would not crack they teeth to them. Finally, the time came for the slave driver to call them to work with the crack of his whip. They come out and they stretch out they hand just like they going to take the tool to work like the rest. But when they stretch they hand they rise. At middle day you could see them far out over the ocean. At sundown you could hear 'o voice, but they couldn't see them no more. Them gone home.[1]

This quote is the reconstruction of a narrative about a group of newly captured Africans on Solomon Legare Island, South Carolina. The occasion of this particular reconstruction came about when Phyllis Green addressed her mistress' question of whether or not Blacks were better off due to the fact that their enslavement delivered them from "the uncivilized state of Africa."

The narrative, as an answer, contains essential components of Black resistance. At this moment of our inquiry, we will be reconstructing and analyzing those essential components within the context of the development of Black political morality. Through these essential components and their historical development, we can begin to reconstruct the development of a moral hierarchy within the Black community and the development of one of the essential building blocks of Black political morality and Black democratic thought.

The first component is the development and the intensity of a collective will to facilitate existence. The Solomon Legare Island narrative locates both the moment of development and the moment of intensity, not only within a particular collective understanding, but also within a particular rhythm. Both collective understanding and rhythm are marked by the relationship between silence and sound as uniquely Black. As with other components of Black political morality, we can inquire into the development of a Black collective will by listening carefully to Black voices. Our inquiry should center upon the intensity and endurance of articulations of resistance. Such an inquiry allows us to reconstruct the development of a Black collective will. Such an inquiry is essential because human will forms the impetus of self-determination.

Virtues such as courage, strength and intelligence are necessary for the development of self-determination. However, these virtues in themselves are not sufficient to facilitate collective self-determination:

> Socrates' simple, straightforward, plain manner of speaking is reflective of *hoplite* virtue. . . . Socrates' method replaces the shrewdness and individual prowess needed in "eristic" argument with traits that promote the benefit of the community—honesty (*Apology* 17A3–B6), the first objective, and seriousness (*Apology* 24C2–7) or stamina required to adequately pursue the truth, the second objective. The third objective makes the *elenchus* something other than a method used in contest with one's fellows and something beyond a method of teaching. For Socrates, *elenchus*, is a hope and investment in Athens' future.[2]

Within this inquiry into Socrates' method of argument, we experience an example of the human will as moderation upon the virtues. Eristic argument, which is geared toward individual success in competition, cannot moderate the virtues, nor does it give them direction, focus. Individual victory stands as the ultimate goal of eristic argument. Within such a narrowly defined goal, competition and abuse are encouraged. Because the will is geared toward such a narrow goal, broad, moderate development is not essential.

The elenchus, as a method of developing and articulating the human will, seeks collective self-determination through resisting individual shrewdness and prowess. In this regard it promotes the equality essential in resistance. Equality is realized through all objectives of the elenchus. These three objectives promote the will as a moderator of the virtues. The will (honesty, stamina and seriousness) is geared toward collective existence, or democratic virtue:

> The *elenchus*, then, is action, beyond speech, concerning things fine and beautiful. *Elenctic* argument is not a win at any cost venture, nor a method which continually stimulates argument and conflict for the purpose of achieving honor. It is a method with the purpose of moving individuals and the *polis* beyond conflict seeking truth through continual rigorous examination and seeking excellence through the care of one's soul. As Vlastos alludes to,[3] since the focus is not competitive, there is no recognizable hierarchical element to the *elenchus*, "everyone is called upon to make perfection of the soul the supreme concern of his or her personal existence."[4]

Socrates' elenchus, then, is a method of institutionalizing the collective will within political discourse. Elenchus is one method of democratic discourse. As a method of political discourse, the elenchus supports the development of democracy in two distinct ways. First it promotes the development of the collective will through discourse, and second it constrains eristic argument that is based on hypercompetitive individual will that often operates outside of the concerns of community.

Black people throughout the Diaspora promote resistance through the oral transmission of narratives and hidden transcripts. Like the elenchus, narratives, hidden transcripts, folk tales and Black music rely upon persuasion not only for the development, maintenance and transmission of values and principles, but also for its own development and maintenance within Black political morality. Like the elenchus, high priority is placed upon honesty, seriousness and endurance, and self-examination within these mediums of discourse. Maybe their most striking similarity is the fact that through these mediums Black artisans, much like the Socrates of the early dialogues, never quite seem to resolve the moral dilemma they place in front of their listeners. Like the early Socrates, they do provide participants with a much greater depth of understanding. The fact that these narratives and hidden transcripts are strikingly similar to Socrates' elenchus in methodological structure is not a coincidence; the similarity results from also serving the functions of institutionalizing the collective will and developing a democratic discourse.

The object of our immediate inquiry is to begin to understand the development of narratives and hidden transcripts, as an expression and development of collective will. The will, at least in Western political philosophy, is neither well articulated nor very well understood. Discourses attempting to define and/or utilize collective will create extensive intellectual conflict, especially in regard to democratic theory. The best-known example is Rousseau's argument of a collective democratic will that at times can only be expressed or understood by a specialized minority.

Western political thought has suffered from questionable methodology, envisioning its own discipline as being driven predominantly by synchronic analysis.[5] Such "static" methodology is not conducive to the articulation and development of experiences such as collective will. Rousseau's difficulty in attempting to understand politics as conflict between the development of a specific historical moral understanding and immediate self-interest is symptomatic of a discipline that understands democracy "as a static, functioning system."[6]

Black political morality, however, in this regard is fortunate. Black scholars have historically utilized diachronic analysis to understand Black politics. Historical context is essential and necessary to the understanding of political experiences such as the development of collective will. As a consequence, collective will is an essential and prominent experience within Black political morality. Reconstructions of a Black collective will are both integral to, and well articulated within, Black political discourse:

> . . . they were tones, loud, long and deep; they breathed the prayer and complaint of souls boiling over with the bitterest anguish. Every tone was a testimony against slavery, and a prayer to God for deliverance from chains.[7]

> The history of the American Negro is the history of this strife—this longing to attain self-conscious manhood, to merge his double self into a better and truer self.[8]

> The spirituals are the record of a people who found the status, the harmony, the values the order they needed to survive by internally creating an expanded universe, by literally willing themselves reborn.[9]

One of the most successful ways in which Black people institute a collective will is through the medium of music. The Black community began to develop music as a methodology of political discourse during the early period of bondage. This method of developing and transmitting the collective will had roots deep within the African experience:

> Black song, of course, had many additional functions both in Africa and America. In Africa, songs, tales, proverbs, and verbal games served the dual purpose of not only preserving communal values and solidarity but also providing occasions for the individual to transcend, at least symbolically, the inevitable restrictions of his environment and his society by permitting him to express deeply held feelings which ordinarily could not be verbalized.[10]

Denied by bondage or other traditional moral and hierarchical institutions, Black Diaspora communities relied upon music much more to transmit complex political understandings:

> Every tone was a testimony against slavery, and a prayer to God for deliverance from chains. . . . To those songs I trace my first glimmering conception of the dehumanizing character of slavery. I can never get rid of that conception. . . . I have often been utterly astonished, since I came to the north, to find persons who could speak of the singing of slaves, as evidence of their contentment and happiness. It is impossible to conceive of a greater mistake. Slaves sing most when they are most unhappy. The songs of the slave represent the sorrows of his heart; and he is relieved by them, only as an aching heart is relieved by tears.[11]

Both Douglass and Levine demonstrate the function of Black music in developing and moderating emotions. The effectiveness of music in developing and moderating emotions along with preserving communal values and solidarity, as Levine notes, is essential to developing the Black collective will throughout the Diaspora. That will, as expressed in Black music, as Douglass notes, is geared towards resisting dehumanization.

At this moment, we need to reconstruct the historical development of resistance in Black music across these historic periods. Levine provides us with an initial template through his analysis of the historical development of Black music and his recognition of at least three dominant forms of Black music: spirituals, gospel and secular (early blues and jazz). We need to begin to understand how each lent itself to institutionalizing Black resistance and the collective Black will. To achieve this, we need to understand the differences in these three forms. Because, at least for Levine, these three forms are representative of three distinct periods of Black historical development and also represent three distinct functions within the Black consciousness, we need to reconstruct the reasons why one form, ostensibly, replaced other forms. Along these lines, we must also further develop Levine's analysis to include soul (60s and 70s rhythm and blues and jazz) and rap music.

We already have discussed what Levine believed was the function of the spirituals. Our next step is to understand why Levine believes the spirituals waned. It would be succinct to argue that Levine attributes the wane of the spirituals to the end of slavery. The end of slavery gradually broadened the worldview of Blacks, individually and collectively. Levine reconstructs this broadening in the divergence of three main forces: education, economics and acculturation. While questioning Levine's reconstruction is not entirely necessary, we should recognize that the divergence of these three forces, however accurate the reconstruction, does not reconstruct the change in the collective will in the Black community.

The other possibility is that there never existed in the Black community the stark division between secular and spiritual, that Levine reconstructs as the basis of his analysis. Douglass, a reliable source of the culture of those held in bondage, posits nothing to indicate the existence of this division that drives Levine's work. In fact, Douglass gives us quite the opposite understanding—that Black people did not envision a separation between secular and spiritual:

> They would compose and sing as they went along, consulting neither time nor tune. The thought that came up, came out—if not in word, in sound;—and as frequently in the one as in the other. They would sometimes sing the most pathetic sentiment in the most rapturous tone, and the most rapturous sentiment in the most pathetic tone. Into all of their songs they would manage to weave something of the Great Farm House.[12]

Again our concern here is not the development of a method of historical analysis, but the reconstruction of the historical development of the Black collective will through music. Our argument is that Douglass' analysis helps us reconstruct that historical development in a more precise manner.

Douglass and Levine do both agree that the environment had a substantial influence upon Black music. We can understand that influence by understanding that the collective will of the Black community sought to moderate the effects of environment. Understanding the changes in the environment is essential to understanding the development of the Black collective will.

The plantation in many ways was a closed environment in which the lines between moral and immoral, good and bad were clearly distinguished, at least for Blacks held in bondage. Levine and Douglass offer us countless examples that give us sufficient cause to believe that Blacks held in bondage understood good and bad, literally, in terms of Black and White. This simple moral structure was superimposed over a more complex moral system, which in many ways exploded the myth of morality and critiqued the sharp dichotomy of good versus bad:

> Similarly, the folk beliefs of slaves were expressed on different but complementary levels. The unremitting system of slavery made its subjects not merely idealists who created a sacred universe which promised change and triumph, allowed them to reach back to relive the victories of the past, and drew them into the rich future where justice and goodness that had been experienced before would exist again; it also made them realists who understood the world as it operated in the present. To have acculturated their children exclusively to a world view proclaimed by their religion would have signified an impracticality that slaves rarely showed. The universe held promise and hope, but it was also dominated by malevolence, injustice, arbitrary judgment, and paradox which had to be dealt with here and now.[13]

Emancipation provided a new context for that malevolent and unjust universe. While the Jim Crow system sought to retain as much of the slavery system as possible, it could not reestablish that closed system. Gradually, those stark, clear divisions between moral and immoral, good and bad, Black and White began to, at least at the boundaries, erode. Gradually the descendents of those held in bondage found themselves in a universe drastically different than that of their parents, grandparents and great-grandparents. The mechanisms of dehumanization were much more fluid and adaptive than those within the closed system. The Black community and individuals within the community began to require a more complex tool to facilitate existence and development. This was reflected in the primary institution available to the community to institutionalize collective will—Black music:

> Changes in religious consciousness and world view are more clearly delineated in the gospel songs, which from the 1930s on displaced the spirituals as the most important single body of black religious music.[14]

The rise in secular music that Levine reconstructs as generally coinciding with the prominence of gospel music is further indication of the development of collective will. In fact, the rise in secular music is indicative of another fragmentation in the collective will of the Black community.

This fragmentation, if we wanted to, at least initially, paint it in its simplest form, is between the political morality held by Booker Washington and that held by William Du Bois. This split was reflective in music and mobility. Levine argues the following of gospel music:

> Jesus rather than the Hebrew Children dominated the gospel songs. And it was not the warrior Jesus of the spirituals but a benevolent spirit who promised His children rest and peace and justice in the hereafter.[15]

Such constituted a simplistic political morality from a historically complex moral and political community. Again we need to understand this as a simplistic layer upon a much more complex moral foundation. To do so we have to analyze a significant moment in Black history. That significant moment is centered around the delivery of Booker T. Washington's 1895 speech before a predominantly Anglo American audience during the Cotton States and International Exposition in Atlanta, Georgia. This speech is known historically as the Atlanta Compromise.

Caution, at this moment, and focus prevents us from beginning our inquiry with a critique of Washington's political ideology. Instead, we seek to understand why Washington's Atlanta speech caused such strong and mixed emotions among Black people. We can begin to understand the development of the Black collective will by analyzing the speech as reflective of a significant moment in Black political morality.

One of the unvoiced conflicts imbedded in Washington's speech is that recognized by Levine as part of the development from spiritual music to gospel music. One way that we can envision that conflict is as part of the conflict between resistance and achievement. The spirituals, in focusing on the warrior Jesus and on the plight of Blacks as similar to the plight of enslaved Hebrew children, stressed resistance. Gospel music stressed achievement (in this life and the hereafter) through Jesus' sacrifice. Washington's speech was explicit in its sacrifice of resistance for achievement:

> The wisest among my race understand that the agitation of questions of social equality is the extremist folly, and that progress in the enjoyment of all the privileges that will come to us must be the result of severe and constant struggle rather than of artificial forcing. No race that has anything to contribute to the markets of the world is long in any degree ostracized. It is important and right that all privileges of the law be ours, but it is vastly more important that we be prepared for the exercise of these privileges. The opportunity to earn a dollar in a factory just now is worth infinitely more than the opportunity to spend a dollar in an opera-house.[16]

While we stay away from arguments concerning the value of Washington's alleged sacrifice of the collective Black will, we can successfully argue that Washington actively sought a particular balance between achievement and resistance. That balance prioritized economic accumulation in regards to equality within an environment. Resistance and the principles and values that the Black community had developed through resistance as foundation of Black political morality were degraded. Washington sought to replace these principles and values with those of Anglo American achievement and secure a place for Blacks within the Anglo American will to control their environment. To accomplish this, Washington was willing to paint a fallacious picture of the Black community and reconstruct an ahistorical understanding of Black excellence. That picture held Blacks up as arduous toilers who were willing to sacrifice many essential aspects of human dignity to participate, in a limited way, in the American dream:

> While doing this, you can be sure in the future, as in the past, that you and your families will be surrounded by the most patient, faithful, law-abiding, and unresentful people that the world has seen. As we have proved our loyalty to you in the past, in nursing your children, watching by the sick-bed of your mothers and fathers, and often following them with tear-dimmed eyes to their graves, so in the future, in our humble way, we shall stand by you with a devotion that no foreigner can approach, ready to lay down our lives, if need be, in defense of yours, interlacing our industrial, commercial, civil, and religious life with yours in a way that shall make the interests of both races one.[17]

This argument was in many ways reminiscent of the American jeremiad that had been adopted by the Northern Black middle class before the Civil War. In Washington's autobiography, *Up from Slavery*, the connections are clear. Washington, in fact, envisions himself as being redeemed by the American jeremiad, crusading Anglo American women who teach him the value of cleanliness, hard labor and self sacrifice in the pursuit of individual and group achievement. The moral hierarchy of the American jeremiad rings clear in Washington's speech recasting the former Confederacy as the Promised Land and reconstructing former enslaved Blacks as the human component of this new Promised Land most willing to sacrifice for its development.

Levine argues that gospel music differed "markedly" from the spirituals because its immediate solutions were a mixture of Christian faith and "one variety or another of positive thinking" and its long-term solutions no longer transcended spatial and temporal barriers, as did the spirituals.[18] According to Levine, gospel music exhibited tenuous connections to humanity's problems:

> ... the gulf between this world and the next had grown wider. There were few songs about the Old Testament heroes, few songs portraying victory in this world. Ultimate change when it came took place in the future in an otherworldly context. Christ, with His promise of a better tomorrow "sometime, somewhere, someday, somehow," was the dominating figure upon whom Man was almost wholly dependent.[19]

This construction of morality, with its limited understanding of collective will and simplistic understanding of Black resistance, fit very much into the construction of the American jeremiad, the Black jeremiad, and Washington's understanding of Negro improvement. We can even go further in our understanding to see that this vision of the Black collective will fit well with the emerging Northern liberal vision (if not a Southern vision) of the United States and the part Black people as a viable source of labor would play in that nation.

While the *resurgence* of Afrocentrism in the 1960s changed, most likely forever, the way the Black community understands Washington (and gospel music), during his era he was popular among a significant portion of the Black population. Many Blacks shared his vision. In fact, the resurgent Black jeremiad predominated among the newly emerging Black middle class, especially the Black middle-class clergy. It was among the Black working class and certain Black intellectuals that the American jeremiad and Black jeremiad faced the most severe opposition, and it is within this section of the population that we begin to see the rise of secular Black music.

The truth is that neither gospel music nor Washington's Atlanta Compromise accurately captured the complexity of the Black collective will and Black resistance. No dichotomous analysis has ever provided the tools to understand that complexity. Such methodologies are much too rigidly constructed. Our alternative is to develop a more dynamic tool of analysis, and one way to develop that tool is to critique the apparently commonsense argument that Black music did not develop primarily as a medium of protest:

> To argue that Negro secular song has functioned primarily or even largely as a medium of protest would distort black music and black culture. Blacks have not spent all of their time reacting to whites and their songs are filled with comments on all aspects of life. [20]

Levine's analysis introduces the possibility of a contradiction with the early statement of Douglass, which imputes that resistance was imbedded in every syllable and note of Black music. Robin D.G. Kelley appears to echo Levine in this understanding by arguing that Black working-class culture was created more for "pleasure, not merely to challenge or explain domination."[21] Kelley's assertion is important because his work is centered on Black music, especially urban Black music.

I believe that this assertion of Levine and Kelley's echoes, rather ironically, a popular passage of Du Bois' *Souls of Black Folk*:

> But when to earth and brute is added an environment of men and ideas, then the attitude of the imprisoned group may take three main forms—a feeling of revolt and revenge; an attempt to adjust all thought and action to the will of the greater group; or, finally, a determined effort at self realization and self development *despite environing opinion*. [emphasis added].[22]

This same understanding appears to be fundamental to C.L.R. James' work on the Haitian revolution, *Black Jacobins*. To add even more fuel to the fire, I would also argue that Levine attaches a historical and generational component to his analysis:

The shifting patterns of black secular music in the twentieth century cannot be attributed exclusively to changing work conditions. Jackson found that many of the younger prisoners refused to sing work songs because they considered them to be "oldtimeyniggerstuff."

Big Bill Broonzy often found blacks in his audiences disturbed by his music. "this ain't slavery no more," he was told, "so why don't you learn to play something else? . . . the way you play and sing about mules, cotton, corn, levee camps and gangs songs. Them days, Big Bill, is gone for ever."[23]

Just as the shift in religious music was related to changes in black thought and life style, so too were the transitions in secular music reflective of alterations in black consciousness and culture.[24]

The essential question, the question on which this conflict turns, is whether or not these changes in the attitude of later generations toward "workaday songs" were indicative of essential changes in the collective will and Black resistance.

The answer is that these changes are more indicative of a fragmentation in that will rather than the broader conclusions that have been posited by many commentators on Black politics and Black music. The most essential reason to found this argument upon is that Black resistance has always been in relation to dehumanization. Policies such as slavery, apartheid or integration are simply methods by which dehumanization as a philosophy and a culture's political morality are institutionalized. The existence or nonexistence of slavery did not alter, has not altered and cannot alter the fact that Black dehumanization has historically formed and continues to form an integral part of Anglo American culture. If this form of oppression were not functional on the level of Anglo American culture, it would not have the strength and endurance to imbed itself so deeply into otherwise seemingly race-neutral political institutions.[25] Black resistance functions to oppose dehumanization; it is not, if it is to be effective, an alternative to American political morality. It is necessarily oppositional at those particular moments when opposition is needed. At other moments it is competitive. Secular music continued in its post-slavery development to fulfill that function. Black music as the primary way of institutionalizing the collective will continued the function and continued it by institutionalizing resistance in the very manner in which it developed within the Black community—upon a cultural basis, infused and inseparable from other aspects of Black life.

It is hard to simultaneously articulate the extent to which understandings such as Levine's and Kelley's accurately reconstruct Black working-class culture *and the extent to which they are inaccurate*. Such reconstructions are only possible, I believe, because of academia. Academic disciplines are able to compartmentalize in a manner that is alien to everyday life. Kelley's work focuses upon an argument that is based on this understanding. However, if it's true that compartmentalization is misleading, then it is not possible to separate the development of culture for pleasure from the development of culture for resistance, especially if that resistance is resistance to dehumanization. One need only recognize the acceptance and cultivation of pleasure as human activities. Granted, it would be nonsense to believe that every time a Black person does something pleasurable they are actively and immediately resisting dehumanization. However, human beings do not reason or act from the specific to the general, but most often just the opposite. In other words, we most often will understand and analyze the general (dehumanization) and decide that we wish to oppose it. As we engage in the specific (our everyday activities) we will most likely, if opposing dehumanization is a priority, examine each specific activity relative to our need to oppose dehumanization. There is no disjuncture between opposition to dehumanization and developing pleasurable aspects of ones culture.

It is not that Kelley's, Levine's and Du Bois' reconstructions are inaccurate; it is simply that in this regard they are irrelevant. Douglass' statement that resistive will is infused into every note, every word, is much more relevant in the sense that it accurately portrays development of the collective will and it portrays the institutionalization of that will in relation to Black dehumanization and *the intensity of Black dehumanization as an Anglo American cultural phenomenon.* Why is this so essential to Black political morality? It is essential because the core foundation of resistance is spiritualism. That foundation is essential so that resistance can be intense and sustained, and yes, consistently oppositional when needed.

This, in turn, is where the danger is encountered. Du Bois recognized the danger as the conflict between Black spiritualism and Anglo American moderate liberalism. While he recognized this conflict, he never found a way to resolve the dilemma—hence the Black double consciousness. Kelley, Levine, even James write within that Black tradition that attempts to reconcile Black resistance with Anglo American moderate liberalism. The truth about Black resistance is that to overcome oppression of Black communities and individuals, it must at essential moments be able to sustain its opposition to moderate liberalism. Such sustained opposition is only available at those essential moments if it is already part of a systematic collective understanding. Douglass recognized this, though late in his career as an abolitionist.

Secular music alone retained the possibility of developing and sustaining a systematic collective understanding of Black resistance that was also practical. Gospel music retained the strength of spiritualism, soul force, but provided it with little direction or focus. Secular music and its development retain the possibility of reconstructing the complexity of the historical development of Black political morality. The ways in which secular music achieves this complexity are through an inclusiveness of most other forms of music—African and European—and its ability to improvise, adapt and balance those forms with the intensity of Black culture.

The complexity began with this ability to amalgamate a variety of different music forms, most notably Black and Anglo American styles, and adapt these styles to fit the Black context.

Improvisational Voices

The most essential and complex aspect of any political morality is the experience of integrating the will of distinct individuals with the will of the community. It is not only the linchpin upon which democracy turns, it is also essential to the survival of nondemocratic systems. In fact, democracy is an argument that the ability to achieve this "reconciling" of individual and collective will is essential to the survival of state and community. It is also an argument that it is best achieved in the least rigid systems.

Improvisation, the skill of creating and performing simultaneously, has been, historically, a primary component of African and Black music:

> The amount of improvisation depends on how long the chorus wishes to continue. And improvisation, another major facet of African music, is certainly one of the strongest survivals in American Negro music. The very character of the first work songs suggests that they were largely improvised. And, of course, the very structure of jazz is the melodic statement with an arbitrary number of improvised answers or comments on the initial theme.[26]

Improvisation did not fade with the waning of jazz as the most popular medium of Black music, although Jones' (Baraka) analysis ends with jazz. Improvisation remained a significant part of Black music in the 1960s (most notably music developed and performed outside the studio). In the 1980s, improvisation formed the heart of the newly developed rap genre. In fact, the development and eventual popularity of these forms are in themselves improvisations within Black culture.

Within a culture that relies so heavily upon narrative for development and maintenance, improvisation is essential. It fulfills functions that are fundamental to that development and maintenance. Improvisation occurs on those occasions that Levine, Jones and others refer to as individuals transcending the restrictions of environment by "expressing deeply held feelings which ordinarily could not be verbalized."[27] Those feelings, as individual voices, penetrate into community bounds—providing context with some flavor. However, we cannot simply dismiss this function as a mere question of seasoning. This penetration is radical movement beyond traditional constraints. Such movement not only retains the possibility of increasing political space, but it functions to make the context more dynamic by constantly applying pressure to even the most transitory understandings of community and tradition.

Improvisation is fundamental to reconciling the individual will to the collective will. The process that improvisation initiates does not end in simple penetration of the individual will into community context, but also requires simultaneously that community context be respected. This is true even in the most radical mediums in which improvisation is intrinsic, such as rap and the dozens. Both of these genres attempt to reconstruct Black communal value systems. Still both must respect historical community values and traditions to be successful. The parameters and values that determine success in any particular game of dozens or rap contest taking place at this moment have been in large part historically determined, sometimes even before the birth of the participants. Jones put it more succinctly:

> As any young Harlemite can tell you, if someone says to you, "Your father's a woman" you must say, as a minimal comeback, "Your mother likes it," or a similar putdown.[28]

One reason why Black culture has historically been so dependent upon narratives is due to the opposition to oppression. Improvisation is not only radical movement; it is revolutionary movement, which cannot be constrained externally prior to its performance because performance and creation are simultaneous. One can think of myriad occasions, such as Stokely Carmichael's cry of "Black Power" or John Carlos and Tommy Smith's raising of Black gloved fists at the Olympics, where improvisation has increased political space by allowing individual Black voices to penetrate traditional U.S. community bounds. While I have used graphic and memorable examples, these are just handy ones. One of the important facets of improvisation as a Black cultural artifact is its historical persistence and the participation in it by individuals on all levels of Black community. In a study of Black narratives, Richard Couto found that improvisation was a large part of the creation and maintenance of narratives, comedy, protest, etc. Couto found not only that this improvisation was essential to the process of developing and maintaining these mediums, but also that it had direct hierarchical consequences because of its direct and immediate penetration into the established Anglo American hierarchy:

> I forget his name but his memory stays with me like the memory of Esau Jenkins. He was smart and he knew how to get things and get things done, even when he didn't have power. One day, right here in Charleston, this old man ran a red light. Drove right through intersection on red. And this cop, white cop of course, pulls him over. He tells him to get out of the car and begins to tell him off and curse him and call him all kinds of names. You know. Well, the old black man, he just stands there and takes it. Finally the cop says, "Boy, didn't you see that light was red?" And the old black man, with his hat in his hand—you never spoke to a white person with your hat on—says, "Well officer, of course I did, sir." And the cop stares at him, amazed. You know. He says, "Then why the hell did you drive right through it?" This time the old black man looks at the cop amazed. Finally he says, real surprised, "Well officer, sir, I thought green meant go for you and red meant go for us." The

cop didn't know what to do and called him some more names and let him drive off. If that happened today, a young black man would start cursing the cop back and argue that the light wasn't red and probably end up with a fine and under arrest. You see, we have to keep alive the wisdom of measuring a situation and getting what we want.[29]

In *Race Rebels*, Kelley experienced similar conclusions:

> While Friday and Saturday nights in Southern cities were moments set aside for the "pursuit of leisure and pleasure," some of the most intense skirmishes between black working people and authority erupted after weekend gatherings. During World War II in Birmingham, for example, racial conflicts on public transportation of Friday and Saturday nights were commonplace; many of the incidents involved black youth returning form dances and parties.[30]

Adaptive and Distinctive Voices

> I consider this less significant because it seems to me much more important, if we speak of music, that features such as basic rhythmic, harmonic, and melodic devices were transplanted almost intact rather than isolated songs, dances, or instruments. . . . The very nature of slavery in America dictated the way in which African culture could be adapted . . . the Negro's way in this part of the western world was adaptation and reinterpretation. . . . But survival of the *system* of African music is much more significant than the existence of a few isolated and finally superfluous features.[31]

> What is significant in all of this is that in spite of their greater exposure to the musical styles of the larger society, in spite of the fact that as the century progressed larger and larger numbers of Negroes could listen freely to—indeed, could hardly escape—the music of the white majority, Afro-American music remained distinctive.[32]

Two necessary components of Black political morality throughout the Diaspora are the ability to adapt and the ability to retain a distinctive voice. These two abilities are necessary because of the lack of resources and the excess of exploitation encountered by most Diaspora populations.

Adaptation is the ability to adapt to an environmental context, to, in a timely manner, become an integral part of the environment. Adaptation is also the ability to change the environmental context, to, in a timely manner, develop the environment to fulfill human needs. Both are essential components of Black resistance.

Distinctiveness, the ability to remain, as a collective, a distinctive voice, is also essential to resisting oppression. It is closely related to adaptation because the will to remain a distinctive force is essential to the ability to change the environmental context. To be distinctive is to resist the power of the environment and other powers within the environment to narrowly define your existence. Since the power to narrowly define one is the power to assimilate in part or whole an entity and its resources, to remain distinctive in any environment entails the will to assess one's own needs and the will to pursue those needs.

To say, in the context of resistance, that Black music is adaptive is to say something that every grade-school kid has been taught, or should be taught. Levine's analysis of the spirituals of Black people clearly chronicles that resistive will to adapt the Old Testament and Old Testament music to fit the Black context. What Levine established is that the foundation for adaptation exists in Black music. That the adaptation was very discriminate is also something Levine argues. Since the adaptation focused on the Old Testament, it allowed Black people to broaden their worldview and develop a resistive self-determination.

The adaptation of songs or even forms of music was only one part of the Black experience; since Blacks were cut off from many cultural resources, the need to adapt other tools to accomplish ones task was evident:

> . . . where the use of the African drum was strictly forbidden, other percussive devices had to be found, like empty oil drums that led to the development of the West Indian steel bands. Or the metal wash basin turned upside down and floated in another basin that sounds, when beaten, like an African hollowlog drum.[33]

Not only, then, has Black culture altered and adapted the goals and form of other music, it has also adapted tools and used those tools to express the Black experience. To achieve a distinctive system of music, with distinctive forms, rhythms and goals, regardless of tools, is indeed a complex endeavor; and is only possible through the development of a complex collective will. The development of such a will is possible through culture, and, arguably, only through culture. It is essential that will is transmitted to politics and implemented within political understandings.

Inclusive Voices

To some extent I believe that Jones, Levine and others have conflated the experience of inclusiveness into that of adaptability. This is primarily due to their focus on musical forms and systems as opposed to our broad focus on political morality. However, for our purposes of understanding the collective will and collective Black resistance, it is essential for us to understand the experience of inclusiveness in Black culture and the distinction between adaptability and inclusiveness.

We have previously considered the experience of inclusiveness in our discussion of marronage. However, in our discussion of marronage we primarily concerned ourselves with the ability of Black culture to be inclusive. We need to extend that discussion to specifically deal with inclusiveness not only as an ability of Black culture, but also as an interest of Black culture; we need to examine the will of Black people to be included within the rest of the human community. We find, at least partially, an inroad to that discourse through Levine's, Jones' and others arguments about the conflict between secular and gospel music. It is a sensitive and complex discussion because it concerns not simply a possible divide between secular and spiritual, but also class divisions.

Levine argues the following:

> Though the slaves' blurred lines between sacred and secular song persisted after emancipation, as I have shown, the decline of the sacred world view inevitably created increasingly rigid distinctions among large number of black religious folk.[34]

Those religiously devout folk envision not only Black secular song as problematic; they also envision nearly every other area of Black secular life problematic. Although Levine's analysis correctly captures the disjuncture between the religious and secular during the rise of gospel, he expends very little energy developing the degree to which class and race played into the development of that rigidity.

In practice, the devout religious folk found the Black secular world objectionable not just because it was immoral, but also because it was Black working-class culture. The devoutly religious never separated the two; they envisioned Black working-class culture problematic because it was immoral and they recognized the immorality because it was Black working-class culture:

> Not o' dem corn shuckin' songs, madam. Nebur sung none o' dem sence I 'sperienced religion. Dem's wicked songs . . . Nuffin's good dat ain't religious, madam. Nobody sings dem cornshuckin' songs arter dey's done got religion.

> Handy's ambitions were similarly dampened at school when he told his teacher he wanted to be a musician. Musicians, the latter informed him coldly, were idlers, dissipated characters, whisky drinkers, rounders, social pariahs. Southern white gentlemen—who should serve as the youngster's models—looked upon music as a parlor accomplishment, not as a way of life.[35]

This circular argument was part of the Black jeremiad. What lay not so deep beyond the surface was the argument of Anglo American cultural superiority. The rigidity, the exclusivity, even within a politically moderate-liberal community, is all too characteristic of American culture, especially in its relationship to Black people. Ironically, most Blacks who adopted this argument did so exactly to be included within the American community. In fact, it is a very plausible argument that their stress on inclusion into the American community as they understood it (or misunderstood it) caused them to draw such rigid lines. In this regard, our previous discussion of Booker T. Washington is enlightening.

The rise of secular music—whether intentionally oppositional or oppositional as coincidence of necessary development—rejected Anglo American superiority, rigidity and exclusivity as matter of both theory and practice. However, the most important question for secular music was not really one of rejecting Anglo American cultural superiority, rigidity or exclusivity. Overcoming those constraints was indeed essential to the primary goal of developing a distinct culture geared toward Black development, specifically a culture in which Black individuals and the collective create and maintain discourses around those interests and issues that inform their humanity. To achieve this, secular music and the collective will that underlay the development of secular music, sought to explore and understand the world around them, as opposed to setting up barriers to keep the world out. This method of development appears to be almost universal throughout the Black Diaspora. Unlike gospel music and the collective will that underlay its development, secular music sought more of a balance between the two types of inclusion. To achieve that balance, secular music was willing to sacrifice immediate gains of appearance for a more balanced development. It was also willing to endure the stereotype of ignorant, lazy and immoral to develop within its own context. The blues and jazz, the two forms of secular music that evolved out of the workaday and disaster songs, were excellent examples of the institution of this collective will:

> Mama and them were so religious that they wouldn't allow you to play boogie-woogie in the house, but would allow you to use the same boogie-woogie beat to play a gospel tune. I just don't agree with this attitude because our music crosses all those lines. Negro music has always crossed those lines.[36]

> In the midst of this environment, young urban jazzmen like the teen-aged Morton absorbed the music and the images of black workers as readily as they learned to imitate the elegant life styles of the millionaires.[37]

> Thus the music and dance of the country and the city, of white and black, of the folk and the commercial music hall, of the church and the street corner, met and amalgamated. At first the musical variations were shuttled back and forth from North to South and city to country by the migratory patterns of so many southern blacks; ultimately the phonograph and the radio played central roles in the constant process of synchronization. The result was that black music had no single locus; it existed wherever Negroes did.[38]

Strong Voices

Thus although blues songs were individual expression they were meant to be shared, they were meant to evoke experiences common to the group, they were meant to provide relief and release for all involved. And, the point is, all present *were* involved, for black musical performances properly speaking had no audience, just participants. It is precisely these qualities that made the blues anathema to so many of the religiously committed.[39]

The blues was threatening not primarily because it was secular; other forms of secular music were objected to less strenuously and often not at all. Blues was threatening because its spokesmen and its ritual too frequently provided the expressive communal channels of relief that had been largely the province of religion in the past. Blues successfully blended the sacred and the secular. Like the folktales of the nineteenth century they had no beginning or end. . . . Like the spirituals of the nineteenth century the blues was a cry for release, an ode to movement and mobility, a blend of despair and hope. Like both the spirituals and the folktales, blues was an expression of experiences and feelings common to the group.[40]

That a culture with the history of oppression so endured would place so high a value upon strength, especially strength of the will to resist oppression, should not come as a surprise. Heroes and martyrs of such a culture are those individuals and collectives who died and lived their lives as the ultimate form of resistance. As Levine indicates, Black culture has produced a pantheon of such individuals, including those of the last generation, Martin Luther King, Jr. and Malcolm X. The production of such individuals and the collective is deeply grounded in the development of the collective will.

While some facets in Black culture—such as the Bad Man tales, toasts, and the dozens—stress individual prowess and wisdom beyond community, strength within the community has more commonly been developed through collective participation and institutions such as the family and church. The fact that music most often plays a large part in these institutions is essential. Kelley, in fact, found the combination of community, youth and music often explosive, arguing that much of the conflict between Black youth and Anglo American authority often occurred as Black youth returned from dances and parties, communal activities centered around Black music.[41]

Collective participation has been key in developing the Black collective will through improvisation, adaptation and inclusiveness. Strength in voices, endless voices, has produced both a distinctive methodology and substantive philosophy within an environment developed to dissuade and prevent such development. The lack of traditional collective coercive institutions, most essentially governing apparatus, geared toward implementing an understanding of a group will has made this endeavor both more precarious and more enriching than similar endeavors developed within more traditional methodologies. Black music, in some sense a peculiar institution by which to transmit political and moral understandings but in context a most appropriate institution, has developed the flexibility, the openness and the strength to facilitate the development, maintenance and institution of a collective will that placed resistance to a hostile environment and hostile inhabitants of that environment as the most essential function of political morality. Without the stress on strength, such a broad and deep attempt at development would have been dissipated long ago:

One ever feels his two-ness—an American, a Negro; two souls, two thoughts, two unreconciled strivings; two warring ideals in one dark body, whose dogged strength alone keeps it from being torn asunder.[42]

The stress on strength in the collective will has been the essential factor in allowing Black culture to be inclusive and adaptive, even in regards to European American culture. Beyond Du Bois' analysis, the stress upon strength and the development of the collective will has been the impetus to propel Black culture beyond such an inherently fragmented existence. What Du Bois understood as a conflict within individual leadership in the 1890s surfaced as a distinguishing feature of the Black community in the decades of the 1960s and '70s. As long as resistance was necessarily the dominant experience of Black political morality, it served in many ways, though not entirely, as a great equalizer within the Black community. It is only after the Black community on the cultural level began to devote significant energy toward achievement that the depths of fragmentation within the community begin to be articulated.

Black Achievement

And of all types and kinds, what can be more instructive than the leadership of a group within a group?—that curious double movement where progress may be negative and actual advance be relative retrogression. All this is the social student's inspiration and despair.[1]

Black achievement in the United States has been, and is, difficult to experience, define and understand. Black achievement is a difficult experience because achievement is culturally defined and developed, but often interpreted as the most individually oriented human activity. The strongest difficulty, however, is inherent in the Du Bois quote above. It is a difficulty inherent in the complex cultural environment in which the Black community finds itself enmeshed. That environment is not only youthful and dynamic, but also ripe with cultural conflict. Much of the conflict has historically centered on definition, redefinition and self-definition of Black identity. Increasingly, cultural conflict is centered on discourses that are internal to the community, such as conflict between competing conceptions of Black development or competing methodologies by which to facilitate that development. The discourse has not only developed from opposing external definitions to developing internal definitions, but that development is reflective of the waning dominance of resistance within Black political morality. As an experience of political morality, achievement increasingly demands a more dominant position within the discourse and the relationship between achievement and resistance become an essential discourse.

In the previous chapters, we have had occasion to reconstruct the development of three distinct strains of Black political thought through the development of Black culture and the experience of Black resistance. It is in the development of the experience of achievement where our reconstruction reaches maturity and our strains reveal themselves as distinct, fully developed traditions within the Black community. Our three strains reveal themselves as traditions because they are grounded in Black culture, and in that grounding demonstrate a historical existence and adherents who consistently access that history to achieve the political goals. Our three strains also reveal themselves as accessible to most individuals within Black culture to the extent that we can envision ourselves through the goals and leaders within each tradition. Each strain exhibits a historical and significant broad-based constituency. Each also exhibits a distinct methodology and distinct goals that go beyond the existence of the tradition. While I do not contend that these are the only traditions within Black culture, I do contend that they are, at this particular moment, the most essential. Other strains of thought, most notably Black feminism, have not yet exhibited the longevity or the historical mass support that each of our three traditions have developed. However, Black culture and Black communities are, I believe, inherently dynamic, and the argument of traditions is one that cannot be closed. By the next generation, other strains in Black culture might well develop into full distinct traditions, especially Black feminism.

To understand the experience of achievement of Black people in the United States, we must begin by looking at the question of why Black people make this transition, that between resistance and achievement, indeed why collectives make this transition. We must also look to the development of our three traditions. It is within each of those traditions that our question of why will be answered, and we can begin to reconstruct the experience of Black achievement.

Transitional Voices

At that moment we left our inquiry into Black resistance, we were discussing the impetus of the collective will and the direction of that will and its importance to the development of resistance. To continue that discussion of the will in the context of achievement, we need to focus on two essential historical components of human activity—collective spiritual activity and collective rational activity. We have already posited spiritual activity as the dominant form of activity in states of collective resistance. At this point, we will posit rational activity as the dominant form of activity in states of collective achievement.

Seeking to understand collective rational activity, we are not concerned with the dichotomy between the rational and irrational that plagues Western political thought. Instead we can define rational activity as collective activity more concerned with developing and justifying a hierarchy of humanness as opposed to being more concerned with ensuring the existence of humans. In other words, our inquiry will now begin to focus upon the political aspect of political morality as resistance previously focused upon the moral aspect. One should understand that we are in no way attempting to develop a dichotomy between two psychological states within individual psyches, but that we are looking at behavior on the aggregate level and positing that certain activities are more indicative of spiritual impetus and certain activities are more indicative of rational impetus. We could easily substitute the word *political* given our definition of rational, but that would not encompass the breadth of the term *rational*. Rational also stands as a term with more depth and history than the term *hierarchical*, exactly because it promotes the possibility of thought beyond hierarchy. Rational collective activity occurs in government institutions, economic institutions, academic institutions and even religious institutions. The essential defining element is the goal of the activity (not necessarily the overall *stated* goal of the institution) to create, maintain and/or develop a hierarchy within an institution and/or among a collective.

The transitional period between achievement and resistance is characterized by heightening conflict between spiritual activity and rational activity. Within that conflict, early forms of achievement are often developed within the spiritual myths of the culture. At this transitional stage, achievement relies heavily upon spiritual myth and spiritual icons to transmit its meanings. The dominance of achievement is characterized by the dominance of rational activity over spiritual activity within the collective.

The question posited is why collectives transit beyond resistance to achievement. Positively, the general impetus for such a transition would be the desire for order, security—the need to aggregate emotions/instincts that develop during resistance but are fleeting. Negatively, humans fear the instability, chaos and lack of security inherent in resistance. Both the positive and the negative necessitate the attempt by the collective to control the environment.

How each collective achieves this control and to what degree they seek to control is particular to populations—particular on the cultural level. The variables that make possible the particular are aggregation and fear. These variables are interrelated. For example, we might posit that the more intense the emotion of fear within the collective, the more energy that collective will expend aggregating emotions that allow them to control the environment. This could manifest itself in the constitutional and institutional arrangements of the collective. Thomas Hobbes partially recognizes this in the development of his dichotomy between a state of nature and state of government. In the Hobbesian state of nature as is so oft quoted, "life is nasty, brutish and short." For Hobbes, government is needed simply to bring order to this chaos. Though some commentators argue that Hobbes' state of nature was a theoretical construct for envisioning the start of government, there is ample evidence that Hobbes believed in the state of nature as a historical necessity. Hobbes' mistake is to believe that at any particular period in human development hierarchy and governing apparatuses do not exist. Obviously, the argument is leading to the assertion that what Hobbes recognizes as a state of nature is simply a state of resistance for any particular collective. Hierarchy is equally present, though not always apparent, in this state. Hobbes' mistake causes him to give his Leviathan absolute power to prevent decline back into this state. Both Hobbes' state of nature and state of government are ruled by a fear of perpetual resistance. Hobbes thinking is historically situated to develop such an understanding. Europe's lingering fear of its medieval period and the colonization of the Americas by Europe created fertile ground for the development and acceptance of such a conceptual construct. On the other hand, we may juxtapose the development of Athenian democracy. The stability of that democracy was based in the development of the *hoplite* or middle-class infantry. Premiums were placed upon bravery and strength. According to Pericles, this tradition resulted directly in a more liberal government.[2] As the strength of the hoplite class fades, however, Athens begins to close its society and centralize power.

At any rate, what we need to understand is that these essential variables develop within specific cultural and environmental paradigms. We can only understand the development of these variables of achievement as rational activity to the degree that a particular collective seeks to control the development of their culture and environment. Since culturally and environmentally specific development defines achievement to such a degree, we must now turn to understanding this specific development within the Black context. To that extent, we need to uncover the particulars of three traditions within the Black community. Of foremost importance, we need to understand how each tradition aggregates its experiences, and what experiences the collective finds most valuable in the process of this aggregation.

The Black Jeremiad

Adherents of the Black jeremiad have historically pursued achievement as integration into Anglo American society. For the most part, they have mirrored Anglo American constructs of achievement in almost every area except one—the development of racial oppression. However, as has been noted in our discussion on resistance, even in this area the Black jeremiad adopts principles, values and understandings of Anglo American institutions. For more than two centuries, adherents of the Black jeremiad have promoted an analysis of Africa and working-class Black people similar to Anglo American conceptions. Similar to Anglo Americans, adherents of the Black jeremiad stress individual competition as the foundation of achievement. In their most vocal context, Black jeremiad institutions have committed the majority of their energy to getting American institutions to uphold the ideals of the American jeremiad through a strict moral reading of the Constitution. In some ways, keeping in mind the noted exception against racial oppression, achievement within the Black jeremiad tradition is in fact as strict, or even stricter than the Anglo American society within which it developed, in its adherence to Anglo American understandings of achievement.

Blacks within the jeremiad tradition began the transition from resistance to achievement clothed in the same spiritual myths as their Anglo American counterparts in the North. They championed the Puritan work ethic, accepted the argument that laziness was immoral, and envisioned excellence as Christian piety that included economic aggregation. As much as with forms of resistance, even more so in achievement, Blacks had no historical context upon which to found these ideals; accordingly, for the most part Black achievement within this tradition became a shadow of Anglo achievement:

> We hence descry some of the grounds for that invaluable importance which has uniformly been given to education, in supplying the mind with intellectual acquisitions, and for adorning it with those elevated accomplishments which have generally been considered as its peculiar fruits, by the virtuous and contemplative of every age and nation; where the genial influences of the Sun of Science have been experienced, and where the blessing of civilized society have been enjoyed.[3]

We have, consequently, part of the answer to our initial question—why Blacks within this tradition transited from resistance to achievement. It was in some real sense an issue of power and resources—a previously enslaved population caught up in the energy of the dominant population. However, this partial explanation really begs the question. The best answer to our initial question lies in the answer to why Blacks within this tradition still choose to shadow Anglo American achievement, which includes the assumption of Anglo American cultural and racial superiority, even though the American jeremiad has proved unachievable and, except within rhetoric, is set aside by Anglo Americans.

Control of an environment is based on a collective's ability to aggregate. The most fundamental form of aggregation is simple population numbers. This type of aggregation was never a state that Blacks of the jeremiad, almost entirely centered in northern states, could hope to achieve. Northern Blacks were a decided numerical minority and due to that numerical deficiency were constantly subject to violent physical coercion by northern Anglo Americans in the form of mobs and state authority. The next form of achieving control is through aggregation of excellence.

Remember that we have split excellence between moral and political. Politics in the United States rests upon three foundations—Anglo American culture, numerical superiority and economic achievement. Morality rests upon Christian understandings and Anglo American cultural superiority. Numerically outnumbered Blacks of the jeremiad attempted control of the environment based upon aggregation of excellence—political and moral excellence:

> People of colour: To you, the murder of Mrs. Cross (a white woman killed by a black man) speaks as with a voice of thunder. Many of you fear the living God, and walk in his commandments; but, oh, how many are slaves of Sin. See the tendency of dishonesty and lust, of drunkenness and stealing. . . . See the tendency of midnight dances and frolics. While the lustful dance is delighting thee, forget not, that "for all these things God will bring thee into judgment."[4]

Imbedded in the answer to how Blacks within the jeremiad tradition attempted to control the environment is also the answer to why they sought control. Given that collectives seek security, leisure and order and attempt to avoid chaos, instability and short life expectancy, Blacks in the jeremiad tradition transit toward achievement to avoid the stigma of an inferior population within an environment controlled by Christian morality and Anglo American superiority. Numerically, Blacks within northern urban and rural areas would be harried (cast into states of resistance) until well into the 1940s. Richard Allen's experience with the Lutheran Church provides an excellent example. It is only through a conscious development of moral and political excellence that northern Blacks can avoid a perpetual state of resistance.

But the rabbit hole gets deeper still. Because the continent and cultures of origin of Black people, Africa and African cultures, were depicted as inferior and pagan, Blacks within the jeremiad could not use any African resources to avoid this state of perpetual resistance exactly because they constituted such a small numerical minority. To avoid a perpetual state of resistance, or, speaking within the language of the American jeremiad tradition, to transit beyond the state of nature, to come in out of the wilderness, this numerical minority needed to excel in Anglo American moral and political cultural norms to gain any level of control within this environment. This includes self-control—hence the irony of a population attempting to gain control of an environment by assimilating into a numerically dominant population. Even more ironic is that this attempt at assimilation included the demand (on itself and the numeric majority population) of maintaining stricter moral and political constraints than those envisioned by the numeric majority population within their own political tradition:

> The Black jeremiad may well reveal the conservative influence of hegemonic ideology upon nondominant groups' public ideas and programs; but it also illustrates the shrewd and art-

ful tendency of subordinate groups to twist and refashion values taught by privileged class-es—even as they accept them—into ideological tools for their own purposes. This fact prob-ably accounts for the Black jeremiad's most distinct and paradoxical trait. The Black jeremiad always strives to speak to and within a changing American social consensus. Yet it is usually at the forward leaning edge of that consensus, prodding it toward evermore thor-ough and inclusive social change.[5]

What a synchronic analysis envisions as "paradoxical," a cultural analysis envisions as enigmatic and untenable, especially in the sense of achievement.

In his statement above, Howard-Pitney affords us a glimpse at the transition-al stage of the Black jeremiad through his initial recognition of the "conservative influence of hegemonic ideology" upon the jeremiad. This influence of hegemon-ic activity is a direct attempt to control the environment. In the Black jeremiad this more often than not took the form of appropriating Anglo American upper-middle-class Christian values. This represents the rational activity of the jeremi-ad. On the other hand, Howard-Pitney's statement also affords us a glimpse at the conflict between the spiritual and rational by pointing us to the jeremiad's "para-doxical state." While accepting the hegemonic ideology, the Black jeremiad con-sistently directs a moral critique at the existing hegemony. Howard-Pitney's statement is couched in terms of the Black jeremiad's energy being directed toward Anglo American society. This in some ways obscures the fact that the Black jere-miad's hegemonic activity and moral critique has been more encompassing in the sense that both have been directed and are being directed at the Black communi-ty. In fact, the demands on the Black community have been historically more strin-gent than those placed upon the Anglo American community. We witnessed this in regards to the Black jeremiad's nonviolent abolition efforts and its simultane-ous economic support of the War of 1812.

This enduring "double standard" coupled with the jeremiad's belief in the development of excellence through Black suffering, which both Howard-Pitney and Henry argue as a significant aspect of the tradition, make this "paradox" much more than a side effect of the ability "to twist and refashion values taught by privileged classes." Instead this activity is indicative of a cultural movement developing a spe-cific philosophical understanding of justice. Such understandings can only emerge out of the conflict between collective rational activity and collective spiritual activity within the tradition. This conflict is reflected in the discourse and lead-ership of the Black jeremiad tradition. Also, a significant aspect of the conflict is defined by the tradition's discourse with other traditions, especially the two remain-ing dominant traditions within the Black community.

Before we inquire into this conflict, we need to understand one more essen-tial aspect of the Black jeremiad tradition. Howard-Pitney speaks of the tradition as speaking with and to "the American consensus." In truth, given the historical connotations of Howard-Pitney's understanding of "American consensus," we find ourselves confronted with an American tradition, and it is to this tradition that the Black jeremiad speaks. To speak within a specific tradition, a tradition that historically celebrates its own superiority, is to be constrained by that tradition. The Black jeremiad is heavily constrained by the philosophical traditions and social/political movements of the American jeremiad. This also means that the tradition's historical movement between resistance and achievement is not self-determinant, but heavily constrained by Anglo American interests.

Our inquiry into this conflict begins in the era early in the development of the Black jeremiad, and specifically the era in which the question of emigration sparked a heightened conflict within the Black community. Both sides of the conflict, those for emigration and those against emigration, were fully imbedded within the Black jeremiad. Both sides still perceived Anglo American culture as superior. In fact, it is questionable if a significant number of Blacks in the United States at the time could conceive of culture outside of European constraints. Most Blacks perceived their African counterparts as unfortunate for not experiencing the enlightenment of European civilization, and saw slavery as a necessary, if overly brutal experience, on the way to enlightenment. The majority of those who went to Africa in any capacity viewed their mission as one of enlightening their African brothers.

One of the most noticeable aspects of the conflict over Black emigration in the United States is the fact that for U.S. Blacks there developed no discourse concerning the spiritual and/or intellectual attachment to Africa, land or people during the first three periods of the question of Black emigration. In fact, it is not until Garvey speaks of aggregation of peoples of the Black Diaspora that such is posited as a legitimate argument for Black emigration. Garvey's argument has never been one accepted, much less posited by the Black jeremiad. The sense in which the Black jeremiad argument connected to resistance is that Blacks within this tradition abhorred the attempt by slave owners and other Anglo Americans to rid themselves of the free Black population, which was viewed by these entities as problematic. Ironically, the constructed identity that Blacks within the jeremiad were attempting to avoid was nearly identical to the identity they themselves held of Africans. This was overwhelmingly the case for Blacks within this tradition before the 1960s. Blacks who advocated emigration exhibited no stronger connection to Africa than those against emigration. In fact, their arguments either supported emigration for purposes of evangelization or purposes of escaping racism. Neither side of the conflict spoke of emigration as achievement through aggregation or through excellence (except in the sense of converting Africa to standards of European excellence). In fact, many saw emigration as disaggregating excellence:

I have been waiting to hear of some way being pointed out that will tend to better the present generation; but, as yet, have heard of nothing that appears to be permanent. I would not wish to be thought pleading the cause of colonization, for no one detests it more than I do. I would not be taken to Africa, were the Society to make me queen of the country; and were I to move to Canada, I would not settle in a colony, but take up my abode in some of the cities where a distinction is not known; for I do not approve of our drawing off into a separate body anywhere.[6]

For the Blacks within this tradition, excellence was represented by not emigrating, which was also closely connected to the plight of Blacks still held in bondage:

Much has also been said by Colonizationists about improving the character and condition of the people of colour of this country and sending them to Africa. . . . We are to be improved by being sent far from civilized society. This is a novel mode of improvement. What is there in the burning sun, the arid plains, and barbarous customs of Africa, that is so peculiarly favorable to our improvement? What hinders our improving here, where schools and colleges abound, where the gospel is preached at every corner, and where all the arts and sciences are verging fast to perfection?[7]

I have attempted to reconstruct particulars of this conflict over emigration to demonstrate that even the questions most closely linked to Africa, the discourse within the Black jeremiad, remained a discourse severely constrained by Anglo American principles and values even in the case of opposition to what was understood as the racist position of the American Colonization Society. The conflict within the tradition between spiritual and rational was decided almost entirely within Anglo American constraints. Though Blacks within the tradition understood the need to transcend oppression, they never equated that with a similar need to transcend Anglo American understandings of excellence. They sought control of themselves and their environment by tightening these constraints upon the actions of themselves and their community. One can only believe that they had so intensely cultivated the possibility of demonstrating their humanity on Anglo American terms that they never did develop a precise critique of Anglo American culture and history.

The site of our next major conflict is the discourse between Booker T. Washington and W.E.B. Du Bois. In the previous section, we placed Booker T. Washington within the Black jeremiad tradition. We also concluded that Washington's political activity was centered upon the goal of achievement versus that of resistance. At this juncture, it becomes prudent to reinforce such an argument:

Then, when we rid ourselves of prejudice, or racial feeling, and look facts in the face, we must acknowledge that, notwithstanding the cruelty and moral wrong of slavery, the ten million Negroes inhabiting this country, who themselves or whose ancestors went through the school of American slavery, are in a stronger and more hopeful condition, materially, intellectually, morally, and religiously, than is true of an equal number of black people in any other portion of the globe.[8]

First, we might want to contrast Washington's argument with that of Ms. Phyllis Green on resistance at the beginning of the previous chapter. Washington's answer to the question stands in direct opposition to that of Ms. Green's. Ms. Green stresses self-determination and the need of the spirit to be free; Washington stresses privileges associated with Anglo American institutions. While spiritualism is the foundation and goal of Green's statement, Washington buries spiritualism under the weight of newly emerging hierarchy and the practical scramble for Blacks to carve out a niche within that hierarchy. For Washington, slavery, the suffering of Blacks through the institution of slavery, notwithstanding the cruelty and moral wrong, has placed Blacks in a better condition in nearly every aspect of human activity than all others of African descent throughout the world. Such is a sweeping claim, obviously problematic. But the academic soundness of the argument is not what concerns us here. Instead we should be concerned with the promotion of the jeremiad theme of Black suffering leading to redemption as the core of the argument. In the jeremiad tradition, Washington attempts to disassociate the oppression of the system from the privilege and benefits of the system. To embrace privilege, he asks Blacks to disregard the loss of more than two centuries of collective self-determination and embrace the very culture that precipitated that loss. In essence, he asks that Black people disassociate morality from religion, and both from politics.

However, there is an aspect of Washington's philosophy and politics that is new to the jeremiad, as Du Bois argues:

> His programme of industrial education, conciliation of the south, and submission and silence as to civil and political rights, was not wholly original. . . . But Mr. Washington first indissolubly linked these things; he put enthusiasm, unlimited energy, and perfect faith into this programme, and changed it from a by-path into a veritable Way of Life.[9]

While each of these aspects of Washington's philosophy and politics fell within the discourse of the tradition, each, according to Du Bois, was marginalized, until their synthesis by Washington. Du Bois also implies that this synthesis is possible exactly because Washington brings to the tradition an emotional energy previously missing. It is not just this emotional energy that Washington infuses into the Black jeremiad. Washington brings with him spiritual resolve, which Du Bois refers to as "perfect faith," that was previously lacking in the jeremiad. However, Washington's faith is not infused into his political thought and action as with Douglass. There is a distinct separation between faith and politics for Washington.

The truth is, in all of Washington's speeches and writings, one would be hard pressed to find passages that give voice to Black spirituality. Washington never experienced the depth of Black spirituals in the manner of Douglass. According to Washington, the war started when he was two or three years old and ended when he was six or seven. Washington appears in his writings to have been very much aloof from the plantation. In his works, there are no tales of friends or advisors within the Black community. More importantly, there is within Washington's writings no significant systematic discussion of any component of Black culture such as the spirituals that hold places of prominence in Douglass' works. The only significant discussion is concerned with depicting Blacks held in bondage as not bitter, quite loyal and even compassionate toward their oppressors. One should find such a discourse extremely problematic, given Washington's youth, the proximity of the war and the fact that Washington had very little knowledge of Black activity beyond his plantation.

Of the perfect faith to which Du Bois alludes, one could say it is similar to the civic faith of Northern Anglo Americans during the age. For Washington, all the elements are present—the protestant work ethic, the equation of morality with cleanliness, the belief that principles and values of the society will overcome individual and cultural forms of oppression and corruption:

> The wisest among my race understand that the agitation of questions of social equality is the extremest folly, and that progress in the enjoyment of all the privileges that will come to us must be the result of severe and constant struggle rather than of artificial forcing. No race that has anything to contribute to the markets of the world is long in any degree ostracized.[10]

Washington's first mentors of note, Mary F. Mackie and General Samuel C. Armstrong, both are grounded in Northern civic religion. Washington during his career is grounded in the civic religion of the American jeremiad. It is a religion that is infused into the civic culture on the most fundamental of levels, but is compartmentalized on the elite level, specifically U.S. politics and academia.

By stressing the most fundamental levels of this civic religion, Washington achieves, at least briefly, a fundamental change in the Black jeremiad. What Washington brings to the jeremiad was to make the philosophy more inclusive and less elitist. This may be the reason that some perceive Washington as a Black Nationalist.

Like the American jeremiad, the Black jeremiad developed a distinctly individual outlook, especially in its pursuit of achievement. Even the political and civil rights of which Du Bois speaks had taken an individual perspective, which, at least later in his career, was part of Du Bois' problem with the jeremiad. Integration as it was conceived, including the Civil Rights movement, was an individually oriented phenomenon in regards to achievement. Washington's attempts to transform the jeremiad into a group-oriented phenomenon were based upon developing individual excellence within this civic religion. However, the cost was the subjugation of the Black populace as a collective. This is the point at which Du Bois contests Washington's politics and philosophy:

> We are training not isolated men, but a living group of men—nay, a group within a group. And the final product of our training must be neither a psychologist nor a brickmason, but a man. And to make men, we must have ideals, broad, pure, and inspiring ends of living— not sordid money-getting, not apples of gold. The worker must work for the glory of his handiwork, not simply for pay; the thinker must think for truth, not for fame. And all this gained only by human strife and longing; by ceaseless training and education; by founding Right on righteousness and Truth on the unhampered search for Truth; by founding the common school on the university, and the industrial school on the common school and weaving thus a system, not a distortion, and bringing a birth, not an abortion.[11]

Du Bois' did not critique Washington from a separate tradition. Even this, his most extreme criticism of Washington, and some of his most spiritually constrained and resistance-oriented work, fits into the Black jeremiad tradition. Du Bois does not oppose the Black jeremiad as a tradition, nor for that matter the American jeremiad, he merely argues instead that Washington has misread the tradition—in fact, misread both traditions:

> To be sure, ultimate freedom and assimilation was the ideal before the leaders, but the assertion of the manhood rights of the Negro by himself was the main reliance, and John Brown's raid was the extreme of its logic. . . . Self assertion, especially in political lines, was the main programme . . . [12]

> In other periods of intensified prejudice all the Negro's tendency to self-assertion has been called forth; at this period a policy of submission is advocated. In the history of nearly all other races and peoples the doctrine preached at such crises has been that manly self-respect is worth more than lands and houses, and that a people who voluntarily surrender such respect, or cease striving for it, are not worth civilizing.[13]

Within the same tradition, Du Bois saw Washington's philosophy and politics as hyperrationale:

> This is an age of unusual economic development, and Mr. Washington's programme naturally takes an economic cast, becoming a gospel of Work and Money to such an extent as apparently almost completely to overshadow the higher aims of life.[14]

In fact, Washington's politics and philosophy mainly concerned the construction and reconstruction of hierarchies on a variety of levels. What Washington also violated, obviously much to Du Bois' chagrin, was the core concept of excellence that previously grounded the Black jeremiad. As previously mentioned, lacking numbers, the Black jeremiad had rested achievement on the pursuit of excellence. Washington's Atlanta Compromise, which Du Bois understood as his adversary's greatest achievement, had nearly overnight changed that locus by threatening to flatten the entire population into a servile caste. Washington reconstructed Black achievement within the jeremiad and founded it now upon the aggregation of numbers:

> One third of the population of the South is of the Negro race. No enterprise seeking the material, civil, or moral welfare of this section can disregard this element of our population and reach the highest success.[15]

> Nearly sixteen millions of hands will aid you in pulling the load upward, or they will against you the load downward. We shall constitute one third and more of the ignorance and crime of the South, or one third [of] its intelligence and progress; we shall contribute one third to the business and industrial prosperity of the South, or we shall prove a veritable body of death, stagnating, depressing, retarding every effort to advance the body politic.[16]

Washington's program, as Du Bois referred to Washington's politics and philosophy, was not overly complex—it sought control through aggregation of numbers (laborers) and the acquisition of capital, or development of an economic base for the Black community. Beyond that it proposed very little. Washington had, in fact, no concept of resistance, physically, spiritually, intellectually, politically or otherwise. His vision began and ended with the concept of Black Achievement. Even that concept of achievement was narrowly tailored—as narrowly tailored as the previous versions of achievement within the Black jeremiad. Du Bois recognized this shortcoming in Washington's work:

> And yet this very singleness of vision and thorough oneness with his age is a mark of the successful man. It is as though Nature needs make men narrow in order to give them force. So Mr. Washington's cult has gained unquestioning followers, his work wonderfully, prospered, his friends are legion, and his enemies confounded.[17]

To say that Du Bois spoke within the tradition of the Black jeremiad is somewhat of an understatement. Du Bois, more than any one individual within the history of Black people within the United States, appears to have approached mastering the tradition. In mastering the tradition, his critique of it is far reaching. In fact, the critique is aimed at Western political traditions (including the American jeremiad) as much as it is aimed at Washington, if not more so.

Du Bois envisioned marrying the excellence that the Black jeremiad had cultivated for more than a century with the resource of numbers that this now second generation of free Blacks in the South represented. He conceived of that marriage in terms of the talented tenth leading and educating Black masses within a democratic society. And while he is only specific about it in the area of the talented tenth, just as much as Washington, Du Bois is intent on reconstructing the political hierarchy within the United States.

Du Bois, as much as Washington, transcends the previous constraints of the Black jeremiad during this period of development. In fact, Du Bois' adaptation and eventual transition beyond the constraints of the jeremiad is most responsible for it becoming a marginalized tradition within the Black community. As Howard-Pitney argued, the Black jeremiad always spoke in the American consensus; in fact, the Black jeremiad had laid so bare the experience of self-determination as to make it seemingly nonexistent. At the time he conceived *Souls*, Du Bois' conception of self-determination was little different:

> To be sure, ultimate freedom and assimilation was the ideal before the leaders, but the assertion of the manhood rights of the Negro himself was the main reliance. . . . Douglass, in his old age, still bravely stood for the ideals of his early manhood—ultimate assimilation *through* self-assertion, and on no other terms.[18]

What Du Bois refers to as assimilation later became more popularly known as integration, and the formal policy goal of the Black jeremiad. This concept of integration directly opposes most experiences of collective Black self-determination, especially if self-determination is culturally constrained as we have argued since the beginning of this inquiry. What Du Bois through the frustration of institutional politics came to realize is that such a conception is untenable. He also understands that the marriage of the elitism of the jeremiad and the culturally distinct Southern Black masses would never work exactly because the conception of self-determination held by the Black jeremiad is untenable. At any rate, as Du Bois attempts to develop a fuller conception of self-determination, he also transits beyond the constraints of the Black jeremiad:

> In the organization whose leadership I shared at the time, I found few colleagues who envisaged the situation as I did. The bulk of my colleagues saw no essential change in the world. . . . My colored colleagues especially were deeply American, with the old theory of individualism, with a desire to be rich or at least well-to-do, with suspicion of organized labor and labor programs; with horror of racial segregation. My white colleagues were still liberals and philanthropists. They wanted to help the Negroes, as they wanted to help the weak and disadvantaged of all classes in America. They realized poignantly the dislocation of industry, the present economic problems; but most of them still believed in the basic rightness of industry as at present organized. . . . [19]

Du Bois who, in *Souls*, arguably develops the most complete conception of the Black jeremiad is ironically responsible for cracking the egg. However, during the conflict, Du Bois remained primarily concerned about democracy and equality. His work, even as he became more concerned with the economic plight of Blacks within the United States, continued to stress the moral aspect of political morality.

While others have argued that the Black jeremiad encompasses most of the development of Black politics and political philosophy, I believe such an argument to be problematic. In retrospect, it appears that the conflict between Du Bois and Washington marks the beginning of a stagnation of the tradition as the dominant political tradition within the Black community. The jeremiad did experience a significant revival immediately before and during the Civil Rights movement due to circumstances surrounding World War II, which included the gradual desegregation of most of the United States. However, within the Black community this revival almost simultaneously stagnated significantly due to various reasons— probably the greatest of which is the large migrations of Blacks into northern and western urban areas and their eventual access to academic institutions in those areas. In fact, as much as we have been able to look at the previous two conflicts as a political discourse within the context of the Black community, we now have to move outside of the tradition to understand at least one side of the conflict, possibly both sides.

While the Black jeremiad has depended much upon American consensus for its rate of development it has been able to develop a systematic understanding of justice that is unique and specific, even in relation to the American jeremiad. The argument of Howard-Pitney that the Black jeremiad is at the "forward leaning edge" of the U.S. political/moral hierarchy is in some sense insidiously correct. The tradition has shaped an understanding of justice based upon the best political and moral understandings within the history of the United States. The strength, and at the same time the weakness, of this conception of justice is that it is based on absolute understandings of ideals such as equality, freedom of speech and individual autonomy, which have never been understood as absolute within the Anglo American mind. In other words, the Black jeremiad has interpreted the ideals within the context of Black cultural development primarily stressing the moral side of U.S. political morality. This is, in fact, the only way that we can truly understand Howard-Pitney's argument that the tradition is at the "forward leaning edge" of a hierarchy that is culturally specific and has consistently rejected the very arguments that Howard-Pitney contends are at its forefront. The historical development of U.S. political thought indicates the problem of such analyses. Americans, while extolling the moral values, have consistently interpreted their own history as stressing the political (or rational) side of political morality.

Few Black political commentators have understood this subtle truth concerning American politics and philosophy. They have either become entrapped in its esoteric articulation of philosophy or its base articulation of "politics as usual." Of those who have envisioned the phenomenon, few have perceived its existence on the cultural level, as a manifestation of the American conception of justice. Even those few still articulate it as a contradiction based on irrational beliefs or failure to uphold standards of justice:

> America has been and still is a nation of freedom *and* injustice. Morgan reminded his read-
> ers that this enduring contradiction prevailed in the consciousness of those who led the
> country into rebellion against Britain in the late eighteenth century. In the same place, at
> the same time, and in the same minds, the utopian dreams of liberty and justice competed
> for right of place with the reality of slavery.[20]

Black Nationalism

We previously identified achievement in Black Nationalism as an aggregation of Blackness. This moment requires us to further develop that analysis. Population growth and ideological development are the cornerstones of achievement in Black Nationalism. Obviously, during the early period of the development of Black Nationalism, there was a need to build population numbers. This was due particularly to the environment in which the tradition developed. Unlike the Black jeremiad, which developed primarily as an elite tradition controlled by Black clergy, entrepreneurs and intelligentsia, Black Nationalism developed as an activist tradition. Historically, those most responsible for developing Black Nationalism have been activists, such as warriors and prophets. These warriors and prophets have forged the tradition primarily through political and moral actions as opposed to written discourse or oral narratives.

The current argument, then, is that the Black Nationalist tradition is developed as an activist tradition. This assertion relocates the locus of the development of Black Nationalism away from the early emigrationists in the United States (who are more properly situated in the Black jeremiad) and fixes the early development within various Maroon communities and the Haitian revolutionaries. In other words, Black Nationalism is not a tradition primarily developed in the United States. It is not that the section of people of the Black Diaspora who reside in the United States have not produced their fair share of activists; more simply it is that those individuals and groups who have contributed most essentially to the development of the Black Nationalist tradition have been from the Diaspora outside of the United States. In fact, we have previously determined that most of the early development of this tradition has come from Maroon communities and the early stages of the development of the state of Haiti. Still, particular periods and actors in the United States have played significant parts in the development of this tradition; the Black Nationalistic tradition has achieved significant development within the Black community in the United States.

We have previously determined that the earliest aggregation within Maroon communities was the aggregation of like-minded people previously held in bondage.

As Fouchard argues, the fact of isolated runaways finding common bonds was inevitable given the hostile environment in which they found themselves.

> We are confronted not with fugitives interested in timid, short-lived escapades, but with
> true rebels—aggressive, determined, and hostile to slavery. What is more, how could we not,
> in all logic, end up with the indispensable complicities, the secret organizations, and the
> hidden networks of resistance to slavery?[21]

Starting as small isolated communities, the first level of achievement was aggregation of numbers. To achieve these ends, they found various ways of recruiting to the extent that they would raid plantations to increase their numbers. However, Fouchard's passage informs us of a distinct quality of Black Nationalism that is present even in its youth, which we cannot overlook if we seek to understand its development. These secret organizations and hidden networks of resistance became the foundation of concise ideological development, which has historically been so essential to Black Nationalism. While this early ideological development appears exclusive or elitist, the secrecy and invisibility is more the effect of an extremely hostile environment than attempts at exclusive control. As the population of the community increases, these secret organizations and hidden networks become more visible exactly because of their need to disseminate their ideology. Black Nationalism operates with the fundamental assumption that most peoples of the Black Diaspora will accept the ideology of Black Nationalism provided with the opportunity to do so. There is no need to control access to an ideology believed to be fundamentally accessible to all. In fact the goal of Black Nationalism and these once-secret organizations is to bring the ideology to a level of understanding (or more precisely, bring the Black masses to a level of understanding) in which Black Nationalism is accessible to most individuals within the collective. We see the inclusiveness of Black Nationalism early in Maroon communities in which these secret societies formed. Because the members of any particular Maroon community often originated from a variety of African ethnic groups, they adapted specific spiritual systems into a more generalized spiritual system that was inclusive of most, to avoid saying all, members of the community. Given the essentialness of spiritualism to the African and Black worldview, this spiritual inclusiveness is important.

One of the initial problems Maroon communities encountered in this pursuit was due to the simple increase in numbers. As these communities grew larger in terms of population, they became less mobile and more visible and in that sense more vulnerable to outside powers that commanded more resources. Maroon communities were faced with either limiting their growth or compromising with external governmental powers. Most Maroon communities whose development fell into the later category all but divorced themselves from the development of any type of Black Nationalist ideology at some point. That disjuncture may have been conceived as temporary or permanent, but most often became permanent. In some respects this type of transition from resistance to achievement is very similar to the reconstruction of the Black-jeremiad transition—heavily constrained by an outside population. Of the Maroon communities that fell into the second category, because they relied on invisibility, very little is known about their early development. But what we can posit from what we do know is that these communities had much difficulty transiting from resistance. In fact, because of their small population relative to the colonial power, they remained predominantly in a state of resistance. This was true of most Maroon communities in the United States.

Given these constraints, only a few communities within the Black Diaspora overcame impediments to the development of Black Nationalism and were able, however temporarily, to develop a systematic understanding of achievement complete with institutions of justice able to implement that understanding. Of these few, the one that is most accessible to us is Haiti. We have previously examined Haiti in regard to resistance; we now want to return to our analysis of Haitian development during its transition from resistance to achievement. The period immediately after the revolution is where we need begin.

Following the revolution, there were two conflicting events that shaped the development of achievement in Haiti. The first event constituted a colonial reaction to the Black revolution. The second event was the development of the Haitian Constitution. These events, from opposite ends of the spectrum, both defined Black Nationalism as a fundamental tradition within Haiti and severely constrained its growth for the next 100 years.

The defining of Black Nationalism as the main tradition within Haitian politics and philosophy begins with the development of the Haitian Constitution. To some extent, our question of why a collective transits from resistance to achievement is answered in a most straightforward manner within this activist tradition. In fact, the need for this transition is most graphic. For the Blacks of Haiti, French oppression created a strict dichotomy between slavery and national independence. Either the Blacks gained control of the environment or they remained in a state of resistance. This dichotomy created between slave and free, European and African, quite naturally influenced the way Haitians conceived of achievement and the development of the Haitian Constitution.

We see that influence in the aggregation of Blackness that is part of the constitution. The constitution, largely due to the influence of Dessalines with strong opposition from Christophe and other mulattoes, effectively defined Black, not on the basis of racial terms, but philosophically as those peoples who believed slavery to be illegal and immoral. Curiously, no previous commentator reconstructs the influence Dessalines' enslavement to a Black slave owner may have played in the development of this definition. Most commentators concentrate on his supposed hatred of whites. But the definition was meant to constrain Blacks as much as whites. Europeans that had continued to fight for Haitian independence with the Black rebels became Blacks with the ratification of the constitution. Reports that Dessalines killed or kicked all Europeans off the island are inaccurate, although he did kill or kick all Whites off the island in the sense that "White" was defined by the Haitians as oppressive and immoral given their support of slavery.

This constitutes the first definition of Black Nationalism articulated on the international level. It predates the actions of Menelik against Italy by almost 100 years. It is also a definition that comes out of an activist tradition. As a definition, it is cognizant of the Black Diaspora:

> Unfortunate Martiniquans, I am not able to fly to your assistance and break your chains. Alas, an invincible obstacle separates us . . . but perhaps a spark from the fire which we have kindled will spring forth in your soul.[22]

In that context, Black Nationalism has always defined achievement through the aggregation of Black people, the aggregation of land, and self-determination or sovereignty. Beginning with the Haitian Maroons and rebels and their ex-slave leader Dessalines, this has always been extremely inclusive, meaning not only all Blacks of the Diaspora, but also Europeans who envisioned slavery and oppression as immoral. This definition also exhibits an intensely exclusive dimension aimed at those Whites and Blacks who envisioned slavery and oppression as fair tools to be used in achievement.

Yet even as this tradition was defining itself, the colonial reaction to the Black revolution had already acted to abort its development. Upon finally deciding to leave the island or when they had feared the inevitable, many of the colonial plantation owners had signed their properties over to their mulatto offspring. This effectively took power over economic development on the island out of Dessalines' and the rebels' hands:

> The sons of the colonists have taken advantage of my poor blacks. Be on your guard, Negroes and mulattoes, we have all fought against the whites; the properties which we have conquered by the spilling of our blood belong to us all; I intend that they be divided with equity.[23]

One reason for Dessalines' eventual assassination two years after the drafting of the constitution was his initial attempt to develop Black Nationalism beyond the state of resistance. Dessalines' story is unique only in the respect that he is the first Black Nationalist leader within the Diaspora to head an independent nation. However, his story, his fate reappears in the life examples of numerous Black Nationalist leaders such as Nat Turner, Malcolm X, Patrice Lumumba and Steven

Biko. Black Nationalism has had rare success in navigating this transitional period and the abrupt ending of the lives of many Black Nationalist leaders' provides
a graphic representation of the harshness in which the tradition has been mired.

With Dessalines gone, Haiti no longer could be defined as fitting within this
activist Black Nationalism tradition. Upon Dessalines' death, Haiti split into separate factions, both led by mulattoes who patterned themselves after European leaders. Christophe and the military gained control of the northern half of Haiti.
Although the northern faction had significantly fewer mulattoes than were in the
south and west, which Petion and a merchant class of mulattoes controlled through
an autocratic civilian government, it was in no manner Black Nationalistic, except
in the sense that it continued the Haitian tradition of abhorring slavery. Petion was
so sympathetic to European Nationalism, especially French Nationalism, that
commentators often accuse him of scheming to place the island back under French
sovereignty—almost exclusively due to his ideological position. Both Petion and
Christophe, like Dessalines before them, abhorred the spiritualism of the Haitian
masses and adopted Catholicism as the state religion. Each also extended
Dessalines' moderate policy of allaying the fears of slave-holding European powers—most essentially the United States.

While their policies diverged little from those of Dessalines, except notably in
the area of land distribution, the policies of Petion and Christophe differed in scope
and goal. One had the sense that Dessalines policies were temporary, the result of
an admitted lack of military resources. On the other hand, one also receives the
sense from Dessalines that his spiritual support of Black Nationalism never waned.
Yet from Christophe and to a greater extent from Petion, one is left with just the
opposite feelings. Blacks by a significant degree outnumber the mulattoes on the
island—all regions of the island. Christophe drew support from an emerging Black
upper-middle-class–aspirant group that controlled the military. Petion maintained
control by pitting the Blacks in the south and west against Christophe's autocra-
cy. He kept Blacks in the west and south divided against those in the north. Both
leaders needed Blacks to rule; beyond that need there appears to be very little personal investment by either in the development of Haiti as a Black state. Maybe
most revealing is the fact that both were willing to allow European powers to inter-
vene into Haitian affairs to maintain control or receive the simplest of advantages.
This type of self-interested leadership set patterns that Haitian leaders and those
aspiring to leadership would adopt for decades leading up to the eventual intervention and occupation by the United States.

However, our concern here is Black Nationalism, and it is within the activist
tradition that Black Nationalism moved, literally and figuratively, out of the
Caribbean, north to the United States, through the vision of Marcus Garvey. It is
essential to note that Garvey did not revert to the resistance stage of Black

Nationalism, but proffered Black Nationalism in its transitional state to a Black population within the United States that was itself beginning to explore the concept of Black Nationalism to a greater extent.[24]

What needs did Garvey Nationalism fulfill among the Black population in the United States? Both Moses and Dawson in their works analyze Black Nationalism and prominent Black Nationalistic leaders as "romantic, self determinate, spiritual, and revolutionary."[25] Such analyses, while in some ways fundamentally flawed, allow us to further refine and develop Black Nationalism as an aggregate and control-oriented activity.

To view Garvey Nationalism as attempting to aggregate self-determination, especially in the 1920–1940s in the United States, does begin to answer our question. We can envision and even quantify this need of self-determination through an understanding of Black demographics during the period. Moses in his academic description of Black migration parenthesizes the need as something well beyond simple pursuit of employment:

> The dominant pattern of black mass behavior from 1876 to 1925 was migration (and enthusiasm for migration) out of the Old South Black Belt. The rhetoric of this migration was often reminiscent of ante-bellum black nationalism, with its talk of escape from the land of bondage and quest for a promised land.[26]

Levine captures this phenomenon much more precisely and in depth:

> Thus the music and dance of the country and city, of white and black, of the folk and the commercial music hall, of the church and the street corner, met and amalgamated. At first the musical variations were shuttled back and forth from North to South and city to country by the migratory patterns of so many southern blacks. . . .

Jones envisions this self-determination in more individual terms as the basis of "primitive blues and primitive jazz":

> The old shouts and hollers were still their accompaniment for the arduous work of clearing land, planting, or harvesting crops. But there was a solitude to this work that had never been present in the old slave times. . . . Each man had his own voice and his own way of shouting—his own life to sing about.[27]

> Creoles like violinist Paul Domingues . . . were expressing perhaps the basic conflict to arise regarding the way the ex-slave was to make his way in America. Adaptation or assimilation?[28]

> And this seems to me an extremely important idea since it is just this bitter insistence that has kept what can be called Negro culture a brilliant amalgam of diverse influences. . . . There was always a border beyond which the Negro could not go, whether musically or socially. There was always a possible limitation to any dilution or excession of cultural or spiritual influences . . . it was at this juncture that he had to make use of other resources,

whether African, subcultural, or hermetic. And it was this boundary, this no man's land that provided the logic and beauty of his music.[29]

Garvey's Black Nationalism and most forms of Black Nationalism that have followed in the United States sought to capture the spirit of that movement, its energy and escapism, and mold it into a nationalist form of self-determination:

> Africa calls now more than ever. She calls because the attempt is now being made by the combined Caucasian forces of Europe to subjugate her, to overrun her and reduce her to the state of alien control that will mean in another one hundred years the complete extermination of the native African. . . . we have pledged ourselves to bring the manhood of our race to the highest plane of human achievement. We cannot, and we must not, falter. There is absolutely no turning back. There must be a going forward to the point of destiny. Destiny leads us to liberty, to freedom . . . that will make us a great and powerful people.[30]

Holistic Voices

At this stage it would appear prudent to begin a categorical analysis of Garvey's development of Black Nationalism and supplement that with a categorical analysis of the Black community's support, or lack thereof, of that development. To begin such an analysis, we need simply start with the following categories: romanticism, self-determination, spiritualism, and revolution. We might change the name of a few select categories to make them more derogatory as many commentators on Garvey have done. Alternatively we may change a few select categories that appear pejorative; such as romanticism to love, as Robin Kelley has done in his analysis of the radical nature of Garvey's Black Nationalism in his recent work *Freedom Dreams*. While I fully agree, especially in the context of how the Black community interpreted Garvey's political thought, that Black love is a more viable and explanatory category than romanticism; I believe that attempts at categorization, while revealing on one level, obscure essential understandings on another level. The other reason to shy away from constructing a categorical understanding is that we need to link Garvey's Nationalism to previous Black Nationalistic understandings in a way that has not yet been achieved. Most emphatically, Garvey himself never attempted such a compartmentalization.

> So Negroes, I say, through the Universal Negro Improvement Association, that there is much to live for. I have a vision of the future, and I see before me a picture of a redeemed Africa, with her dotted cities, with her beautiful civilization, with her millions of happy children, going to and fro. Why should I lose hope, why should I give up and take a back place in this age of progress? Remember that you are men, that God created you Lords of this creation. Lift up yourselves, men, take yourselves out of the mire and hitch your hopes to the stars; yes, rise as high as the very stars themselves. Let no man pull you down, let no man

destroy your ambition, because man is but your companion, your equal; man is your brother; he is not your lord; he is not your sovereign master.[31]

In his leadership, Garvey harkens us back to the early Maroon community leaders. He is imbued with both political and spiritual energy and attempts to imbue
his followers with that same energy. Garvey's speeches consisted of political arguments founded upon a particular conception of God. In Garvey's conception, God
was Black and redeemed Black people and a Black empire—if Black people sought
to redeem themselves. As Moses argues, Garvey's conception of religion falls close
to his Catholic upbringing.[32] Not having been raised in the tradition of Black
churches, Garvey understood the energy of spiritualism somewhat differently than
the Haitian Maroons or even Dessalines, his activist Black Nationalistic predeces-
sors. Even Dessalines, who adopted Catholicism as the official state religion,
understood spiritualism as energy within the physical world. Garvey didn't follow
such an understanding.

To be fair to Garvey, two centuries of being required to operate within Western
tradition had affected the worldview of most Blacks within the Diaspora. Spiritual
energy was seen primarily as having only a psychological force. Garvey, however,
still perceives of spiritualism beyond the psychological, and understands the connection between moral energy and political energy:

> The call to Africa is still more than the indefinable cry of an oppressed people, more than
> the interpretation and the inspired utterances of a bold and inspired leader, whom the Negro
> acclaims, who spreads discomfiture among the ranks of Negro oppressors; the Call to Africa
> is the voice of the Omnipotent. Let my people go, that they might serve me. The Call to
> Africa is the Omnipotent in the act of delivering His people from bondage. . . . Three hun-
> dred years of unparalleled horrors reaching down to the atrocities of the Belgian Congo and
> still intolerable conditions prevailing to this very moment could not but move the Heaven
> of Justice to vindicate her Cause. . . . Slowly and surely the arm of Omnipotence has been
> outstretched to bring justice to the Negro. His is now passing through the Red Sea wall. His
> day of victory is at hand.[33]

Garvey's synthesis of politics and spiritualism, while it is developed on the level
of existence similar to the early Maroons and Dessalines, avoids the direct physical connection between spiritualism, leader and group. The early Maroon leaders
and Dessalines were associated with a spiritual energy; this energy was directly transmitted through leaders to the group, affording the group spiritual and physical protection. As many commentators have concluded, this understanding of spiritualism
is part of most African traditions. What abounds in Garvey's speeches is an interpretation of the Old Testament. However, that interpretation is more indirect and
impersonal than the spiritualism of early Black leaders, the Maroons, Dessalines,
even Douglass. For Garvey, spiritualism is primarily psychological—the correct spir-

itualism uplifts the race through developing ambition, lifting the race from an imposed inferiority that is the cause of laziness, individuality and depression:

> I believe with Napoleon. When some one asked him "on what side is God?" he replied. "God is on the side of the strongest battalion." Napoleon was right. He had a true concept of God. God is really on the side of the strongest peoples because God made all men equal and He never gave superior power to any one class or group of people over another, and any one who can get the advantage over another is pleasing God, because that is the servant who has taken care of God's command in exercising authority over the world.[34]

This particular passage comes from a speech entitled "God as a War Lord." In the speech, Garvey envisions an active God who is a "bold Sovereign—A Warrior Lord," as well as a "God of Peace."[35] Like the Old Testament construction of Blacks held in bondage, Garvey constructs a warrior God. However, Garvey's similarities with the worldview of Blacks held in bondage ends with his depiction of God. Man is alone, stands alone, whether he is righteous or not, to determine his own fate upon the planet. Neither God nor spiritualism imposes upon humanity a directly intervening force.

In Garvey's conception, spiritual existence simply acts to honor already existing power. Where they have value to the oppressed is in helping them to understand that all men have an innate power that they simply need to develop, in fact, have a mandate to develop as God's servants. In Garvey's understanding, spiritualism is power, and God who nurtures power in humanity intervenes only to recognize power. Garvey's conception is obviously hyperrational, relegating morality as useful only in the cultivation of power. Garvey's concern is with the aggregation and control of power—power based upon a religious psychology that envisions all groups, classes and races as equals and places them in direct and indirect competition to take up "God's command in exercising authority over the world." What is not being aggregated, that which Garvey has no interest in aggregating, is any sense of right or righteousness. In this Garvey's synthesis of power and spiritualism is, as Kelley argues, radical. It is also, in comparison to most Black understandings, pared down in the area of spiritualism.

While his worldview lacked a fully developed understanding of Black spiritualism, Marcus Mosiah Garvey developed Black Nationalism to a degree not previously achieved, especially in connection to the Black masses. This is primarily due to his synthesis of politics and Black love, or what many of his commentators have referred to derogatorily as romanticism, narcissism or megalomania. Garvey, as E.U. Essien-Udom describes him, was a Pan-African Nationalist.[36] Although he held understandings of Africa that were similar to those of previous Pan-African leaders, most notably the responsibility of Blacks throughout the Diaspora returning and uplifting Africa into modern civilization, there are distinctions to Garvey, especially in his synthesis of power and Black self-love. In some ways, this is best understood in terms of who—Garvey understood as an asset in uplifting Africa and who—he understood as a detriment in this endeavor:

> It is hoped that when the time comes for American and West Indian Negroes to settle in Africa, they will realize their responsibility and duty. It will not be to go to Africa for the purpose of exercising an over-lordship over the natives, but it shall be the purpose of the Universal Negro Improvement Association to have established in Africa that brotherly co-operation which will make the interests of the African native and the American and the West Indian Negroes one and the same, that is to say, we shall enter into a common partnership to build up Africa in the interests of our race. . . . The Negro has had enough of the vaunted practice of race superiority as inflicted upon him by others, therefore he is not prepared to tolerate a similar assumption on the part of his own people. . . . It will be useless, as before stated, for bombastic Negroes to leave America and the West Indies to go to Africa, thinking that they will have privileged positions to inflict upon the race that bastard aristocracy that they have tried to maintain in this western world at the expense of the masses. Africa shall develop an aristocracy of its own, but it shall be based upon service and loyalty to the race.[37]

In the remainder of his speeches, Garvey does much to develop this dichotomy between selfish, jealous, bombastic elitism and brotherly love within the masses. It is a dichotomy that drew popular sympathy, if not direct support from the Black community. This dichotomy, however problematic, exposes two popular sentiments within the Black community. The first sentiment is the connection to Africa and the peoples of Africa, which Garvey develops throughout his speeches. As we have previously determined, such connections were not made in early forms of Pan-African Nationalism, including those developed by Cuffe, the infamous American Colonization Society, Delaney or Crummell. The UNIA with Garvey as leader, as Kelley argues, is the first to construct understandings of Africa as the motherland. In fact this is a primary construction within Garvey's famous "Africa for Africans" speech.[38] While Kelley picks up this argument in context to gender, another essential context lies in Garvey's distinctive vision of Pan-African Nationalism. Garvey presents an Africa and African people that can be embraced exactly because they are Africa and African, as opposed to being an escape or a place upon which to imprint frustrated elitist ambitions.

While Moses argues against many commentators' perception of Garvey as a mass leader based on the fact that Garvey did not see all Africans returning to Africa, it appears through the construction of his dichotomy that Garvey is actually seeking to discourage elites (or those with elitist aspirations) from returning to Africa, not the masses. This understanding is consistent with Garvey's bitter conflicts with U.S. Black and West Indian leadership and his understanding of their shortcomings. The ignorance that Garvey attacks appears to be limited to the ignorance of elites. He appears to believe that the problems he finds within the masses can be addressed through adherence to a correct religion and the development of self-confidence and Black self-love.

The second sentiment is that of Black abhorrence of exploitation. We have previously encountered the strength of this sentiment in the actions of the Haitian Black masses toward Toussaint L'Ouverture. As C.L.R. James claims, the Black masses were willing to throw over Toussaint when they suspected that he was not firmly behind the ending of their exploitation. This, after all, historically is the leading reason for the development of Pan-African Nationalism from its earliest conception up to Garvey. In previous conceptions, that abhorrence of exploitation is only articulated in one sense—the escape from exploitation by the United States as a racist society. In Garvey, the articulation of part of the Black experience becomes more complete in the sense that it is not only articulated as an abhorrence of being exploited, but also as an abhorrence of exploiting others.

Yet Garvey's conception of Black Nationalism is aborted much in the same way as is Dessalines' earlier attempt at popular Black Nationalism within the activist tradition. The abortion of Dessalines' form of Black Nationalism takes place due to an elite faction of privileged landed mulattoes who both fear and loathe Blacks and Black political control of the island, and an upwardly mobile faction of middle-class blacks who seek expanded wealth. Garvey's Nationalism falls due to bitter friction between himself and other non-nationalistic Black and West Indian leaders, who have also been accused of being middle-class aspirant, and certain factions within the Anglo American population who fear the development of widespread Black political power. In both cases, these factions conspired to keep proponents of Black Nationalism landless and leaderless.

Still, Garvey struck a chord by institutionalizing these two sentiments. That chord continues to reverberate within Black Nationalistic thought and Black political thought. That chord was incorporated into the Black Nationalism developed through the Nation of Islam by two leaders within the Black activist tradition—Elijah Muhammad and El-Hajj Malik El-Shabazz (Malcolm X). It is to this development of Black Nationalism that we now turn.

In both form and spirit, the Nation of Islam took up Garvey's grassroots philosophy and organization methods, which appealed to the Black masses. One could literally say that Elijah Muhammad, the founder of the Nation of Islam, took his message to the streets and recruited his followers from the streets, expanding on Garvey's theme of developing the masses and severely critiquing Black elite leadership. Muhammad, like Garvey, recognized that those most capable of articulating and developing Black Nationalism in the context of Black achievement would come from the faction of the population that most opposed other formulations of achievement. Malcolm X rewarded this recognition, after first being recruited by the Nation of Islam in prison, by becoming one of the most prolific and popular leaders within the history of the Black community in the United States. Maybe more important for our inquiry is that Malcolm X, like Marcus Garvey, reconstructed Black Nationalism philosophy as an essential component within the popular worldview of the Black community. This has not been achieved since by any Black Nationalistic leader; and it is not simply due to the supposed impracticality of Black Nationalism, but because no Black Nationalist leader has had either the resources or intellectual energy to achieve such a conception on the community level.

Militant Voices

Only a dead Malcolm X is available to young people today. . . . He has no dynamic connection to the lived reality of the youth who invoke him. He is grafted into their world of experience as a frozen icon to be revered, a reification of other people's memories. This Malcolm X does not encourage by providing a running critique of the prevalent narrative of oppression as it evolves. . . . To that extent, today's Malcolm is marked for and by objectification. . . . Yes, it is ironic that Malcolm—whose appeal in life was linked in so many ways to being militantly *un*fashionable—has become a fashion statement.[39]

What Malcolm's narrative shows us (unintentionally, at least) is the capacity of cultural politics, particularly for African-American urban working-class youth, to both contest dominant meanings ascribed to their experiences and seize spaces for leisure, pleasure, and recuperation. Intellectuals and political leaders who continue to see empowerment solely in terms of "black" control over political and economic institutions, or who belittle or ignore class distinctions within black communities, or who insist on trying to find ways to quantify oppression, need to confront Ellison's riddle of the zoot suit.[40]

These statements, juxtaposed, in many ways capture the difficulty of understanding Malcolm X as a Black Nationalistic leader. Not only do the statements drastically oppose one another in the significance of Malcolm X's political thought, neither statement correctly situates that thought within its proper context—Black Nationalism. In fact, in both Reed's and Kelley's understandings (both devote at least a discrete chapter of their work to understanding Malcolm X), very little is mentioned of Black Nationalism. Reed speaks of Malcolm almost entirely as a Black radical, and Kelley for his part reconstructs a radical Malcolm through his early participation in Black urban working-class culture.

Both arguments concerning Malcolm X exhibit some in-depth understanding of the connection that Malcolm makes among the masses and his development of political thought through activism. However, neither argument analyzes the connection, nor the activism through the context of Black Nationalism. This is in some ways understandable for Reed, who seems to be in a hurry to disavow Black

Nationalism as a legitimate form of politics (despite its obvious popularity within the Black community); but it is less understandable for Kelley, who exhibits no particular animosity toward Black Nationalism. While Reed's fault lies in not listening to the voices of a significant Black political movement through his desire to reduce Black Nationalistic thought to "fashion," Kelley's fault lies in ignoring the voice of the Nationalist Malcolm X, the Black leader who envisioned his participation in the Black working-class culture not simply through the context of the "civil rights movement and a resurgent Pan-Africanism," but through the context of an oppressed member of a Black community pursuing its freedom and humanity.

Obviously, our immediate task becomes one of giving space to both voices in the context of a developing Black Nationalism. The importance of this reconstruction goes well beyond addressing either commentator's shortcomings. The real truth is that Malcolm X's most essential contributions to the development of Black Nationalism are exactly the things that these commentators and most commentators on Malcolm X overlook or critique. In this, Malcolm X suffers the same historical fate as most Black Nationalists, especially Dessalines and Garvey—despite their overwhelming support of the masses, in connection to other forms of Black political thought, they are marginalized within Black history.

There is an irony in Reed's argument concerning the stylishness and lack of style of Malcolm X as a Black Nationalist leader. That irony must first be reconstructed through race, class and cultural privilege. One can begin to conceive the irony that Reed unconsciously reconstructs in the sense of Malcolm X's political thought being embraced by himself and members of his "cohort," because it was "unfashionable." Kelley successfully argues that it is only unfashionable in the sense that it is a Black working-class phenomenon, and that at the time the Black working class was unfashionable outside of its own environment.

Whether it is associated with the conks and zoot suits as Kelley does, or the afros and leather jackets as does Reed, Black Nationalism and especially militant Black Nationalism as a form of Black political thought and as a Black political movement has gathered little popularity outside of the Black working class. It has indeed a continuing history of being unfashionable with the Black middle class, whether located in the Caribbean or the United States. It is both a valid and rhetorical question to inquire if the unpopularity of the Black working class itself (outside of its own environment) exists for the same reason. On the one hand, we could make an argument that Reed is referring to the co-opting of Black Nationalist thought and the allure of Malcolm X by Anglo American institutions. However, this really hasn't been done, and even if it were true it is not what Reed is referencing. Reed's reconstruction centers on the popularity of Malcolm X with Black inner-city youth; and to the degree that he refers to Malcolm X as fashionable or unfashionable, he is measuring Malcolm X's popularity and unpopularity among that group.

The fact that he then reduces the popularity of Malcolm X among inner-city youth to a consideration of fashion represents his precursory awareness of the political understandings of working-class Black inner-city youth. Kelley anticipates such arguments. Kelley recognizes the energy of empowerment in Malcolm's contest with dominant meanings. Kelley's genius is to recognize that what Reed refers to as fashionable is the method of Malcolm X and Black Nationalism becoming an essential component of Black culture. When this is understood, one recognizes Reed's irony in decrying the fashionableness of certain components of Black Nationalism and Malcolm X as a Black Nationalist leader.

One also should, through the construction of this argument, understand that one essential achievement of El-Hajj Malik El-Shabazz to the development of Black Nationalism is the institutionalization of Black Nationalism within the Black community through essential principles and values of Black culture. One way of conceptualizing this is that the model of Black strength that Marcus Garvey sought to develop through an Afrocentric psychology El-Hajj Malik El-Shabazz is largely responsible for institutionalizing on the cultural level. This redemption of Black, as Kelley refers to it in his latest work, is in truth more than redemption. It is a form of catharsis in which the values and principles of working-class Black America, which oppose various constructions of American capitalistic oppression/privilege, are exposed as beneficial because of their ability to continually facilitate existence and development through the medium of Black Nationalism.

One should readily understand the need for catharsis within a culture that has historically developed their opposition to oppression/privilege on the level of narratives and hidden transcripts. As Kelley recognizes in his analogy of the riddle of the zoot suit, it is Afrocentrism (through the medium of Black Nationalism) in transition, a celebration of the hidden becoming seen, the faceless distinguished—at any rate, it is the acceptance of Black working-class culture as a viable culture that, like all cultures, maintains the primary function of facilitating the existence of its adherents. In many ways it is a celebration, although relatively low key in nature, of the existence of Black. Malcolm taught us that we could survive as Black, Black as we defined Black. This pursuit of Blackness, one's humanity, is the goal of most inner-city youth, and historically the goal of the community. The fact that in some rhetorical quarters it is presented as fashionable should not, does not, deter young Blacks from its pursuit.

We have given Malcolm X much credit for developing this; however, the truth is that many hands went into this development. Malcolm X in correct context, places the impetus of that popular sentiment within Black Nationalism. Historically, it belongs there.

The second essential achievement of Black Nationalism through the leadership of El-Hajj Malik El-Shabazz is the redemption (more accurately, partial redemption) of Black working-class culture. Again Kelley in his work *Race Rebels* through a strong historical analysis has perceived the foundation of this redemption—the catharsis of Black working-class urban culture. In this Kelley has surpassed those who envisioned Black inner-city culture as "outlaw or nihilistic."[41] Still, Kelley's vision suffers from its own shortsightedness with Black Nationalism:

> But Malcolm's narrative of his teenage years should also be read as a literary construction, a cliché that obscures more than it reveals. The story is tragically dehistoricized, torn from the sociopolitical context that rendered the zoot suit, the conk, the lindy hop, and the language of the "hep cat" signifiers of a culture of opposition among black, mostly male youth. According to Malcolm's reconstructed memory, these signifiers were merely "ghetto adornments," no different from the endless array of commodities black immigrants were introduced to at any given time. Of course, Malcolm tells his story from the vantage point of the civil rights movement and a resurgent Pan Africanism . . . [42]

Kelley recognizes the redemptive value of Black Nationalism in his next work *Freedom Dreams*.[43] Still, that recognition is mostly with Garvey and the UNIA and mostly on the theoretical level. There is no concrete discussion such as found in *Race Rebels* and certainly no discussion connecting Malcolm X's life to redemption through Black Nationalism.

Even a historically problematic form of Black Nationalism such as that originally formulated by the Nation of Islam provided certain principles of discipline that assisted in the development of Malcolm X and many other Black inner-city working-class youth. It is that discipline through which we also view his and their lives. Again Garvey conceived it in terms, not very concrete, of a Black psychology, at the center of which lay a strong Black religion. The first step to any institutionalization is the development of a discipline. Disciplines often begin with fundamental constructions and develop into much more complex structures.

At the beginning of my undergraduate studies, I had the fortune of going to see Minister Louis Farrakhan speak at a local college. It was a few years before the popularity (and unpopularity) of Farrakhan had spread to the West Coast, so I was one of the few in the audience and had a seat in the front row of a virtually empty auditorium. The speech, as much as any rhetorical instrument could, took on a lot of properties of a seminar. I remember at the time Farrakhan's discussion constituted a critique of Black inner-city working-class culture. Even as an undergraduate, I found it to be somewhat ahistorical. For instance, he began speaking about popular terms such as *baby, crib, mama*; terms used in intimate relationships between Black males and females, and argued that this was a reflection of the immaturity of Black culture. While Farrakhan also connected this to slavery in the sense that such meanings were imposed upon Black people by Anglo American culture seeking to retain its dominance, an argument opposed by this very work, the larger message I took away from the event was that a Black inner-city working-class culture as strong and as beautiful as I experienced it needed to further develop in particular areas.

For Malcolm X and other Black inner-city youth, the discipline of Black Nationalism provided at least an impetus, at most a methodology, for further development. Black Nationalism as a methodology of development proved essential for the redemption of Black working-class culture. This redemption is much more in-depth than previous commentators have envisioned, exactly because most reconstructions of Black working-class culture, especially as it is conceived in its inner-city environment, have depicted it as nihilistic and/or outlaw.

At this moment it becomes sufficient to introduce this argument. Its proper place, however, is within the next section, on our third tradition within Black political thought. As I have mentioned earlier in the introductory chapter, El-Hajj Malik El-Shabazz went beyond the constraints of Black Nationalism; in that context the redemption of Black working-class culture belongs within the third tradition.

The truth is, the focus of Black Nationalism moved beyond the confines of the United States with the assassination of El-Hajj Malik El-Shabazz, the rise in power and prominence of Black African nations and the struggle for power between Nationalism and quasi-colonialism within those arising Black African nations. Within the United States, Black Nationalism has not advanced significantly beyond the state of transition. Its aspirations remain frustrated, and often that frustration is focused on the Black community.

Cultural Pluralism

> Despite appearances of consent, oppressed groups challenge those in power by constructing a "hidden transcript," a dissident political culture that manifests itself in daily conversations, folklore, jokes, songs and other cultural practices.[44]

Kelley, an excellent historian, reveals much in this passage. Despite excellent commentary in the area, hidden transcripts have been applied indiscriminately to the Black population as a whole. Such an argument would necessitate the development of hidden transcripts across at least our three traditions. However, in our examination of our previous traditions, we have seen little occasion for either tradition to develop a hidden transcript. The Black jeremiad has always operated within a written context. Black Nationalism has forged a strong activist tradition. For either, hidden transcripts would be unnecessary and, in some real sense, counterproductive.

Instead it is our third tradition that has developed primarily through the medium of narratives and hidden transcripts. Thinking in terms of historic development and goals that distinguish an elitist written tradition such as the Black jeremiad from a tradition driven by narratives and hidden transcript, the difference is somewhat self evident. It is only between Black Nationalism and cultural pluralism that distinctions become somewhat blurred. We have previously distinguished the two traditions in a very general manner, pointing to one as cultural and the other as activist. Such a distinction is too tentative, one dimensional and incomplete. The fact is that activism and cultural development at the most fundamental of levels need not be mutually exclusive.

The ultimate distinction is within the goals of these traditions. We have previously revealed these disparate goals and the conflict between these goals in our earlier discussion of the Haitian Maroons. The fundamental goal of Black Nationalism has always been the acquisition of power by Black people—individual, discrete groups, the collective. However, Black Nationalists have never really understood power as culturally defined or ethnically specific. Instead they have perceived the importance in the hand that has wielded the power. Toussaint's beliefs and principles fell along this line.

The Haitian rebels, whose political consciousness rested upon the foundation of the Maroon colonies, had as a distinct goal the eradication of oppression—not just the transition of power into Black hands. They clashed with Toussaint exactly because he was willing to compromise the former for the latter. Even as Dessalines was able to fulfill the promise of Black Nationalism in Haiti, the differences between the ex-slave general and the rebels, despite essential similarities, were striking. Dessalines, like the Haitian rebels, abhorred most forms of oppression and it appears would not have accepted any permanent power arrangements that did not include liberty for the Blacks. Yet there is a point of conflict between him and the rebels at the level of culture. Unlike most of the rebels, Dessalines, had distinct problems with Voodoo, the dominant form of Haitian spiritualism that developed as an amalgamation of various forms of African spiritualism.

Yet they held on to Dessalines, as much as they had previously held on to Toussaint, despite this significant difference. As long as Dessalines' politics supported Haitian cultural development and opposed most forms of oppression, the two traditions did not clash—in fact, were very much compatible. Unlike Black Nationalists, cultural pluralists have shown little concern for who (in terms of race and ethnicity) holds the reigns of power as long as the regime and system is compatible to their cultural development. In the United States, this has meant the promotion and development of cultural pluralism. This, along with its medium of development, distinguishes Black cultural pluralism as a unique tradition.

Unlike Black Nationalists who understand Blackness as an ideology or philosophy, cultural pluralists experience Blackness as culture. While philosophy may well develop out of principles and values essential to a particular culture, culture itself is much more dynamic, much broader and more energetic than philosophy. In the case of Black culture, that dynamic nature during times of severe oppression has always been transmitted through narratives and hidden transcripts. It was labeled dissident by its oppressors exactly because the interests of oppressors oppose the development of an independent culture among the oppressed. Oppression has as one of its essential goals the dehumanization of the oppressed. Why indeed do slaves need to tell stories, to marry, to worship? The only positive answer to slave owners is: if it makes them more productive chattel. Narratives and hidden transcripts develop as opposition to the dehumanization—the fact that they are encoded on the cultural level is essential.

The transition between resistance and achievement for Black cultural pluralists is probably the most easily recognizable among the three traditions—the increasing visibility of narratives and the hidden transcript. This increasing visibility is indicative of an aggregation of culture and cultural space—traditions, principles, norms, institutions—as a form of achievement. It is not merely aggregation that develops during this period of transition, it is also a coming of age for Black cultural pluralism. This coming of age is demonstrated by the development of maturity and excellence in distinct areas of Black culture, the most essential of which are the redemption of Black cultural forms, rejection of the arguments by Western philosophy of the inferiority of Black and African culture, the contest for space (both political and physical) with other cultures within the Black Diaspora and the catharsis surrounding these developments.

In resistance, cultural pluralists develop a discourse that promotes cultural principles, values and norms distinct from Anglo American culture. That it has been the only non-Anglo collective of significant size to do so is still a point of conflict within the United States. That it has been the only Black political tradition to do so is why it has remained "hidden" in "folk" narratives for so long. It also explains, or at least partially explains, why the tradition and the extent to which Black people are part of the tradition is hidden within other Black political traditions.

As resistance, cultural pluralism took the form of what Kelley refers to as "infrapolitics":

> I use the concept of infrapolitics to describe the daily confrontations, evasive actions, and stifled thoughts that often inform organized political movements. I am not suggesting that the realm of infrapolitics is any more or less important or effective than what we have traditionally understood to be politics. Instead, I want to suggest that the political history of oppressed people cannot be understood *without* reference to infrapolitics . . . [45]

Infrapolitics forms the core of the political discourse within the Black community during periods of resistance. This community-based discourse informs Black people of the virtue or lack thereof within other political discourses, forms a critique to competing conceptions of humanness. Its existence is at the most fundamental level of collective human activity—culture.

The problem is that throughout the history of the Black Diaspora, this discourse, as Kelley brings to our attention, has been considered "dissident." Fouchard envisioned the attack on this discourse, as did Fanon, in much more insidious terms. Both of these commentators recognized the attempt of mainstream Anglo American discourse to derogate the development of Black culture to an individual phenomenon and then classify the individual phenomenon as *spiritually and psychologically abnormal behavior*. Hence those who fought against slavery by running away were not necessarily political dissidents, but "lazy" or "evil-doers." This is indicative that the fundamental conflict between Blacks and Europeans existed at the cultural level, not the political or economic level. As we look deeper into the Black psyche, we will find that this is the reason why other political discourses are in whole or essential parts rejected by the Black community—including Marxist discourses.

How does a discourse mature and develop excellence within such a hostile environment? The answer to essential components of that question lies, ironically, in volatile events that caught Anglo Americans and many Black leaders by surprise during the last three decades. These events are usually referred to as Black urban riots or rebellions and are usually analyzed as if they are idiosyncratic to northern urban "ghettos."

Most commentaries have perceived riots as forms of resistance against various real or imagined oppressors. For example, the McCone Commission, which undertook, with government resources, a detailed study of the Watts riot, concluded that: "rioters were marginal people and the riots meaningless outbursts."[46] Fogelson, in his critique of the McCone Commission, concluded that the rioting in Watts was conducted by a significant portion of the Black population and was due to apathy caused by governmental and societal oppression. The riots constituted resistance to this oppression. Fogelson also blamed the riots on Black leaders and "the absence of a distinctive Negro culture in the United States."[47] As have other commentators who've come after Fogelson, Harris attempted to put the riots into perspective within a cultural context. To these commentators the riots are properly "rebellions" against oppressive political (mostly police) and economic tactics of Anglo American society.[48] Henry, in his work on Black culture and politics, concludes that two groups participated in the Watts riots: "those who rioted for a specific set of grievances and those who rioted for fun and profit."[49]

Each analysis proceeds from the assumption that resistance was the primary impetus for rioting, or in the case of Henry, legitimate rioting. Ironically, while all these analyses are problematic it is Henry's that is most illuminating. While we may ultimately conclude that Henry's simple dichotomy does not capture the complexity of Black political behavior, it does reveal that angry, spontaneous, reaction to oppression, if indeed it was a motive for rioters, was not the only motive. A statistical study of rioting by Olzak, Shanahan, and McEneaney reveals that "patterns of residential segregation and desegregation are more central to understanding race relations than issues of Black poverty or racial disparities in income."[50] What the researchers found was that the potential of Black unrest increased with the increase of racial *competition* (White intervention) within Black communities:

> In other words, we expect the breakdown of segregation or *apartheid* to incite racial unrest when and where segregation barriers have previously existed.[51]

What Henry and Olzak and her co-authors point to is the problem inherent with concluding that Black urban riots and/or rebellions are primarily motivated by resistance. Commentators who attempt to analyze riots predominantly as acts of resistance encounter nearly as many problems as those who attempt to analyze riots as outbursts of marginal individuals. The last problem that most commentators have incurred is that of classifying riots as predominantly political or economic. Possibly the most revealing analysis of Black activity during inner-city riots is that which begins to envision them as rebellions of cultural pluralism. Riots also must be analyzed as an essential period of transition between states of resistance and achievement. This becomes evident in both quantitative and qualitative analysis of the event and the people. What these analyses lack is an essential historical context for both people and event.

Physical violence in the Black Diaspora is historically associated with the transitional period from resistance to achievement—aggregation and gaining control of oneself and the environment. They are not the initial stage of organized activity for oppressed peoples. In fact they are necessarily the final stage of organized activity. One does not expect to engage in physical violence with the mere goal of continued existence except in extremely desperate situations. Most situations of physical violence, except such cases like that experienced by Frederick Douglass in his fight with Covey, begin well past the endurance of the most desperate hours. Most of the individuals responsible for planning and directing rebellions within Black history have been individuals who in relation to others within their oppressed group have accrued some type of well-defined privileges either from resistance to the system or cooperation with those who control the system:

The leaders of a revolution are usually those who have been able to profit by the cultural advantages of the system they are attacking and the San Domingo revolution was no exception to this rule.[52]

Toussaint fit neatly and graphically into this mode, as did Rigaud, the mulatto leader. James, of course, was only half correct because the Haitian rebels were also constituted of a large number of Maroons. The Maroons, under the leadership of Mackandal and later Boukman, took no cultural advantage from the colonial regime.[53] The privilege that these individual leaders—and by extension, the Maroons in general—had forged was in opposition to the system. However, it was nevertheless privilege, or achievement, in relation to the oppressed group, those still enslaved. These men, Mackandal, Boukman, Toussaint and Rigaud, pose serious questions for political analysis. The most serious of questions is even though the Haitian Revolution is depicted as a revolt that ended slavery on the island, it was not started by those who were enslaved at the moment of the first spark of the revolution. Instead it was started by those who had previously liberated themselves and had indeed forged a history of raiding the system to increase their resources. In other words, it was a war over control of the immediate environment. Nor was it on the part of the Maroons started as a defensive war to protect the liberty previously acquired. It was initiated to elevate the community beyond a bare state of existence, an act of controlling environment.

We have previously, with the help of Moses, made the argument that the popularity of Garvey's form of Black Nationalism was due in large part to the development of Harlem. Harlem provided a center for Black activity that was not available before the large migration of Blacks from south to north. We now have occasion to make the same argument concerning the Black cultural renaissance that very early was centered in Harlem. Harlem constituted a forerunner. The fact is most inner-city urban areas became bastions of Black cultural development during the 1960s.

It was not that the South did not develop a distinct Black culture; in fact, this is far from the case, as we have previously discovered. Southern patterns of oppression constrained that development to certain forums, especially particular collective forums. The system of Southern apartheid accomplished a couple of essential things in regard to Black culture. First, it kept Black culture out of public spaces, except in very minute ways. By disempowering Blacks politically, the system severely constrained development of aggressive components of Black culture, especially components that develop in dynamic forums. It goes without saying that the Southern system of slavery, which evolved into the system of apartheid, attached a stigma of inferiority and illegitimacy to Black culture. What is not so evident is that the Southern system was essential in the development of divisions within the Black community over the question of Black culture:

As the outside culture became more visible and accessible in the twentieth century, the dilemma grew. The *lames* might be laughed at within the group, but it was they who often had the better chance of mobility and success outside. Negro children were hardly socialized to the vernacular of their own group before they learned of its disadvantages and low status in the larger culture. Thus for black Americans as for other minority groups in the society, the socialization process increasingly became a dual one: an attempt to learn to live both within and outside the group. In language as in so many other areas of black culture this has produced a broad and complex spectrum.[54]

While Levine appears to be discussing American society in general, in fact his discussion is limited to the South. Levine is writing about the post–Civil War period, when more than 90 percent of the Black population remained in the South. Levine indeed casts doubts on the existence of a strong distinctive Black culture outside of the South prior to the migration of a significant number of Southern Blacks into Northern urban areas. Here he argues that Southern Blacks migrating to the North were perplexed by Northern Black traditions:

> De [Blacks] heah ain't got no Holy Spirit and dey is singing no 'count songs—dese white songs from books."[55]

When the large migration wave (during the 1920s) reached Northern urban areas, they met a small group of Blacks led by a small but aggressive and entrenched Black middle and upper class. Most of this class also had a decidedly Anglo American bias in regard to culture or had pretensions in this direction.

However, public spaces were relatively open, especially so in Black communities such as Harlem. This openness was essential to the ability of Black culture, which previously developed hidden transcripts and narratives as the predominant mediums of cultural transmission, to move beyond these mediums to more bold and aggressive forms of cultural transmission. This development obviously did not occur overnight—however, it did occur across the span of two generations.

The first stage of that development was an aggregation of numbers. The migration waves, during the 1920s and 1940s, allowed Southern working-class Blacks to quickly outstrip the small dominant entrenched Black middle and upper classes in numbers. Numbers transmitted to political and economic power, and maybe more important, to development of cultural and political pluralism centered in inner-city Black communities, of which Harlem became the jewel. There was much more that added to the development of Black cultural pluralism, such as the emergence of independent Black African nations and the Civil Rights movement, which was at the forefront of at least the rhetoric of ending segregation and developing equality within the United States. But the foundation lay upon that movement and the aggregation of Black people and the continuing desire (whether explicit or implicit) to develop a unique and distinct Black culture. The distinctiveness of Black culture was not simple opposition to Anglo American cultural forms. Opposition to these forms did exist; however, that opposition was grounded in particular understandings of excellence. That particular form of excellence had been developing for nearly two hundred years when the last migration wave had become firmly entrenched in inner-city communities throughout the North, West and even within the South.

Competitive Voices: Voices of Excellence

The historical truth is that neither the methodology of the Black jeremiad nor of narratives and the hidden transcript is conducive to the development of excellence in the area of Black cultural pluralism. The Black jeremiad promoted excellence within a particular cultural paradigm that was antagonistic to the development of Black cultural forms; narratives and hidden transcripts operate on the level of existence and are developed with the goal of cultural survival. To a great extent, both the Black jeremiad and Black Nationalism were sought to submerge the question of culture within questions of politics and economics. The result of this submergence was to place "practical politics" at the forefront of the Black struggle at the expense of more philosophical concerns. But the migration waves had placed these philosophical questions at the forefront of the struggle; and as Harold Cruse recognized, they presented both opportunity and misfortune to Black leadership, which was mostly grounded in either Black Nationalistic or Black jeremiad traditions:

> As long as the Negro's cultural identity is in question, or open to self-doubts, then there can be no positive identification with the real demands of his political and economic existence. Further than that, without a cultural identity that adequately defines *himself*, the Negro cannot even identify with the American nation as a whole . . . *thus it is only through a cultural analysis of the Negro approach to group "politics" that the errors, weaknesses and goal failures can cogently be analyzed and positively worked out.*[56]

The fact of Black existence placed these philosophical questions not only at the forefront of Black cultural development but in competition with, at least, the Black jeremiad as a political tradition and the larger context from which the Black jeremiad evolved, Anglo American culture. It is in this competition that Black cultural pluralists began to develop standards of excellence and began to lift those standards to a level of maturity.

Although Cruse is the first to significantly articulate this problem and although other commentators since Cruse, such as Henry in his work on politics and Black culture, have attempted to develop analyses within this area, the first work to address the essential problems in this area has been Robin Kelley's *Race Rebels*. At this moment, we need particularly concern ourselves with Kelley's analysis of Black working-class youth culture through the mechanism of his analysis of Malcolm X and rap music.

Kelley brings our attention to the level of competition, the pervasiveness of the competition and the stakes of the competition. He also informs us that the competition is grounded in cultural forms. While on the one hand Kelley informs us of competition at the level of culture, Levine informs us of the moral foundation of this alternative understanding of excellence—an amalgamation of fragments of African philosophy and Old Testament theology. While most illusions to this amalgamation speak to the connection between Blacks as slaves and the children of Israel, we should not lose sight of the prominence that justice and just moral law has within the Old Testament.

> This unique subculture [Black working-class culture] enabled him [Malcolm X] to negotiate an identity that resisted the hegemonic culture and its attendant racism and patriotism, the rural folkways (for many, the "parent culture"), which still survived in most black urban households, and the class-conscious, integrationist attitudes of middle-class blacks.[57]

Kelley is correct in arguing that Malcolm X was able to develop a unique identity within Black working-class culture. However, everything that Malcolm X does within this culture, and everything that Kelley analyzes of this "subculture," indicates that it is not in resistance to other cultures but in competition with them. This competition took place on every level of culture. Kelley captures that competition in the area of clothes, music, style and leisure:

> By March 1942, because fabric rationing regulations instituted by the War Productions Board forbade the sale and manufacturing of zoot suits, wearing the suit (which had to be purchased through informal networks) was seen by white servicemen as a pernicious act of anti-Americanism—a view compounded by the fact that most zoot suiters were able-bodied men who refused to enlist or found ways to dodge the draft. Thus when Malcolm donned his "killer-diller coat with a drape-shape, reat-pleats and shoulders padded like a lunatic's cell," his lean body became a dual signifier of opposition—a rejection of both black petit bourgeois respectability and American patriotism.[58]

Kelley also captures that competition on the collective level:

> The sight of hundreds moving in unison on a hardwood dance floor unmistakably reinforced a sense of collectivity as well as individuality, as dancers improvised on the standard lindy hop moves in friendly competition, like the "cutting sessions" of jazz musicians or the verbal duels known as "the dozens."[59]

He also reconstructs the complexity of that competition as an interaction of interests between different facets of the Black community and their desire and need to engage Anglo Americans on economic and political levels:

It should be noted that the music itself was undergoing a revolution during the war. Growing partly out of black musicians' rebellion against white-dominated swing bands, and partly out of the heightened militancy of black urban youth—expressed by their improvisational language and dress styles, as well as by the violence of looting we now call the Harlem Riot of 1943—the music that came to be known as "bebop" was born amid dramatic political and social transformations.[60]

While most commentators remark on the social nature of competition within the Black community, and while those engaged in these competitions for the most part are energized more by their participation as opposed to dominating their fellow competitors, one distinct goal of competition in the Black community is excellence. Development of excellence is achieved by encouraging both participation (being as inclusive as possible as discussed in chapter three), improvisation and by placing winning as a distinct, if not ultimate, goal of competing.

We have previously reconstructed this understanding of excellence as a necessity of resistance; we now have necessity to reconstruct how it is promoted as possibility of achievement. Black movement into inner-city urban areas was not simply for survival. Those moving out of the South sought first and foremost control (to the greatest extent possible) over their own life chances. This was as true on the collective level as it was for most individuals. As a group, Blacks pooled their resources to promote movement (Black newspapers were often at the forefront, though word of mouth proved effective), they often threw rent parties to assist one another with expenses; in fact, they (despite commentaries to the contrary) brought their cooperative culture to these areas intact. I have had numerous occasions to discuss with students some of the more humorous and interesting facets of being raised by an entire community. The patterns established in resistance became patterns for achievement.

Black culture, which had previously, for purposes of survival, relied on amalgamation, adaptation, inclusiveness, improvisation and a particularly pronounced will, *began to celebrate these virtues and the interaction between them developed into a distinct understanding of excellence.* The goal of that excellence, as Du Bois argued, was twofold—to overcome racism and contribute to the historic excellence of humanity. These goals were not seen as mutually exclusive; in fact, they were perceived as inherently compatible. More specifically they are attempts to control the immediate environment.

Even at that early a moment in Black history, Du Bois envisioned that excellence was already being conceived as cultural pluralism within the Black community. Du Bois, as did most commentators after him, also understood that cultural pluralism as a goal retained the possibility of contradicting the way the goal was to be achieved—through competition. In all of the competitive activities listed as analyzed by Kelley—style, dance, music—the competition retained the possibility of first diverting the ends and then becoming an end in itself. In fact, we see this with power in Black Nationalism, indeed all forms of nationalism, and with the American ethos, in the Black jeremiad.

The concept that presented a possible contradiction to the method of developing and instituting excellence was one that had developed out of the experience of intense opposition to, and, indeed abhorrence of, oppression. This to, I would argue, became an essential component of the pursuit of excellence within Black cultural pluralism. This is the point where cultural pluralism most identifies with the Black jeremiad and is weary of the power-dominated rhetoric of Nationalism and Marxism. It is also the point where cultural pluralism contributes something entirely new to the history of political thought—the conscious development of a concept of excellence that is moderated by an experience of intense racial and cultural oppression.

We now can return to a more direct discussion of the riots. As much as Black culture engaged in contests with other cultures in the areas mentioned above, it also engaged in contests over physical, political and economic territory. Many commentators have described these contests to be over hegemony in those areas, while other have described the events as resistance for reasons listed in the preceding paragraphs All of the studies, once we take into account the historical development of Black cultural pluralism, point to the fact that the riots were not simply resistance against oppression but part of the transition of a culture between states of resistance and achievement. Yes, the violence did occur out of frustration. However, the frustration developed not only due to oppression at the level of existence or to attempts to resist dehumanization, although this played an essential part of the development. Instead, for most Blacks, the riots were also, maybe even predominantly, about the quality of life and an integral part of cultural competition.

What the various studies on rioting cannot quantify is the fact that the portion of the Black population that had moved into inner cities during the great waves of migration had done so mainly for increased economic and social opportunity. Much of what underlies the McCone Commission's conclusions that Blacks were frustrated with the police and that only marginal Blacks engaged in the rioting was the belief that Blacks formed a naive immigrant population that was not used to large-city political, economic and social institutions. To a large extent this was supported by the testimony of established middle-class Blacks. Two things drove this assumption. First, Anglo Americans in the North and West perceived themselves as strikingly different from Southern Anglo Americans. Second, they believed that Blacks just up from the South shared this viewpoint but were suspicious due to the repressive history of the South. Both were false and unbelievably arrogant assumptions from the perspective of Black people.

The fact was the population that migrated to the North was hardened by American history, skeptical and extremely determined. They had already experienced the impersonal as well as personalized racism of Anglo American institutions; most of the migrants, former service workers such as housekeepers, gardeners, cooks, had experienced intimate contact with Anglo Americans. Most were aware, or became aware through the Black community network, of the *historical* discrimination against Blacks in the North and West. They also understood the political, economic and social subtleties of America very well. They were, in fact, an experienced population trapped into an immigrant niche and historically socially constructed within the South and North as culturally inferior. As Cruse noted, they understood the American dilemma well:

> On the face of it, this dilemma rests on the fact that America, which idealizes the rights of the individual above everything else, is in reality, a nation dominated by the social power of groups, classes, in-groups and cliques—both ethnic and religious. The individual in America has few rights that are not backed up by the political, economic, and social power of one group or another. Hence, the individual Negro has, proportionately, very few rights indeed because his ethnic group (whether or not he actually identifies with it) has very little political, economic or social power (beyond moral grounds) to wield.[61]

This was evident in the conflict between police and the Black community. While many commentators have concluded that Blacks perceive the police as an occupying oppressive force meant to contain crime within inner-city Black communities, the more precise understanding of police that abounds within the Black community is that of corrupt referees within the cultural contest. In truth, most people in inner-city communities expect nothing more from White policeman as low-level civil servants who are employed to enforce cultural disparities. The pejorative "pigs" captured this understanding in multiple dimensions. Later pejoratives such as "dogs" extended the understanding.

In fact, the clashes between the police and young Black males and females are border clashes—marginal engagements at the fringes of both societies. These marginal engagements always have the potential of erupting into full-scale battles over contested territory. The territory in question has always been misunderstood by most commentators. They have envisioned it alternatively as physical, economic, political or social space. Very rarely have they envisioned it as cultural. However, all evidence supports the conclusion that the terrain in question was and is cultural. The gist of the problem is obvious—politics, economics, social mores, are all subsumed under culture. Given the Eurocentric model of academics, however, it has historically been considered problematic to study a phenomenon such as culture—it is believed to be too broad. Still, in the midst of the chaos of the rioting, the only clear understanding that can be drawn without ignoring some essential body of data points to cultural conflict.

The truth is that migration, which was about economics, politics and free movement, had added the *experience* of freedom and self-determination to Black culture. It was in everything and quite naturally Blacks wanted more. Especially within Black communities, individuals and the collective alike moved in it, breathed it, were nourished on it, came to know it as both concept and experience, but most of all came to feel it on the level of culture. The Black mind was expanding, and with it, Black culture.

Anglo American society represented, had historically represented, an impediment to that development. It had always represented a series of hurdles for Blacks on their way to cultural development. This hurdle, this experience, Blacks also understood on the level of culture, understood it as a feeling. These two feelings were distinctly different and in some ways diametrically opposed—one an intricate set of steps, twists, leaps to a deep intricate beat; the other toil, knee-deep in mud, stooped, bent at the waist under a hot sun, picking, picking, picking . . .

This was the cause that formed the foundation for the riots. Rioters understood game, players and stakes. The violence, looting, property damage were part of the transition between resistance and achievement—the hidden transcript becoming an in-your-face aggression. For cultural pluralists at these particular moments, the choice is straightforward:

> "Let's cool it!" he said.
> "Man! Where you from?" one challenged him.
> You from the west side? From Baldwin Hills?"
> "No man," Dymally answered, "I live here."
> "You must live in some big house."
> "No man. I'm with the people."
> "If you're the people—" the kid handed him a bottle,
> "Throw it!"
> "No man. I'm for peace!"
> "Hell!" the kid said. "You with the *man!*"[62]

The truth is that the population that had endured the migration found themselves in a chasm between a former lifestyle of daily resistance and that of aggregating that which was necessary for achievement. Political and economic power were within reach of Black communities—vast numbers had afforded Blacks some form of political strength in such communities as Harlem and Watts, the Black middle class had visibly begun to grow, although incrementally (in fact, Baldwin Hills at the time was home to a number of wealthy Blacks, mostly in the sports and entertainment industry)—however, Blackness was still disparaged, still inferior.

So the riots represented for the rioters among other things an aggressive action, a purging of unsolicited entities from their impoverished communities. Anyone unwilling to throw the brick was part of an unholy alliance, or with the man. Peace was subjugation, and allowing oneself to be once again mired in resistance. The intuitive knowledge that led to the riots was straightforward. It was the knowledge that resistance alone is not a sufficient state of human existence.

Institutional Voices

Fundamentally, institutions are collections of individuals who seek to achieve some specific goal within society. Normally, these individuals find pooling their resources a distinct advantage in achieving their specific goal. The goal can be broad, such as social justice, or narrow, such as one individual's economic interests; however, for the goal to be institutionalized it must be, narrow or broad, achievable through collective activity. Because pooling resources forms an essential component of institutions, acquisition of resources become an essential function of the institution. One of the most salient features of institutions is the fact that unless the goal of the institution is distinctly the interest of one individual, then individuals and individuality are subordinate to collective interests. This, however, should not be mistaken to mean that institutions are democratic by nature; individuals involved in institutional processes simply find collective action more conducive to achieving a particular goal. Instead we may want to think of institutions as the crystallization of particular understandings, values and/or principles within a given culture.

In this section we are concerned with the institutionalization of essential tenets of our three Black political traditions. While we do not have the time or space to develop a complete history of institutions within each tradition, we do have the ability to develop a generalized history that will reveal some specifics of development within each tradition. These specifics will be uncovered so that in the following chapter we can understand how conflicts have arisen between the traditions and how these conflicts may be bridged.

Black Jeremiad

Institutions within the Black jeremiad developed earlier than institutions within our other traditions. As a consequence, Black jeremiad institutions are much more specific (narrower in goal and constituency), varied and numerous than institutions within our other traditions. These institutions historically are concerned about securing the rights of Black people within the United States context. One might argue that these institutions have been concerned about integrating Blacks into the larger society. The basis of that integration has been the American jeremiad.

Given that fact, Black jeremiad institutions are grounded in Anglo American culture and have an essential stake in the prosperity of the United States. However, the most salient feature is their primary goal of uplifting the Black race.

The strategy by which they seek to uplift the race is based upon embracing American principles and values and demonstrating to Anglo Americans that Black people can become virtuous, productive citizens and good neighbors within a predominantly Anglo American community. In retrospect, one might argue that early institutions within this tradition were primarily concerned with two things: first, the end of slavery; and second, the integration of Blacks into American society. Following the emancipation, the latter became the most essential political purpose of these institutions. They appeared, not unlike the Anglo American institutions at the time, obsessed with developing among their members and the rest of the Black community a strong moral foundation—this they believed was necessary for uplifting the race. Consequently they were obsessed with dispelling the Ham accusation (the argument that Black people were cursed by God and skin color was evidence of that curse), the savage-heathen accusation, and placed great constraints and pressure upon individuals within the community to successfully integrate into the Anglo American ideal: Booker T. Washington.

The Civil Rights movement was the culmination of the intellectual, political and spiritual voices of the Black jeremiad. The concept of uplifting the race through the agitation for rights had been the goal of three major institutions. First, the NAACP, which in the nature of its founding epitomized the goals of both the American and Black jeremiads, and championed full citizenship rights for Blacks through the courts and politics. Second, SCLC, championed full citizenship rights through moral suasion in the form of nonviolent protests. Third, Black colleges and universities provided the intellectual paradigm and an army of intense, committed youth that was essential to the development and political activity of the two previously mentioned institutions. What lay within the grasp of these institutions was the complete revamping of American concepts of justice. However, this promise was never fulfilled, partly because voices within the Black jeremiad never recognized until very late in the day that asking most citizens to abide by the letter of their own constitution, without it being in their determined best interests, is politically radical.

In part the Civil Rights era waned within the Black community because of this fundamental contradiction within the institutional voices of the Black jeremiad. Black jeremiad institutions preached American mainstream, but ironically remained on the margins of American society. In fact, as Anglo Americans envisioned the ends of the Civil Rights movement, as they became wary of moral suasion, these institutions slipped further toward the margins.

Black Nationalism

The existence of Black Nationalistic institutions within the United States remains problematic. As an institutional phenomenon, Black Nationalism has been encouraged, hunted, infiltrated and marginalized by the U.S. government. No other attempt to legally organize political institutions has been so highly scrutinized by official government entities as has Black Nationalism. Maybe because of the above, or maybe it is merely coincidental—whatever the reason—Black Nationalistic institutions have been organized and/or led by some of the most visionary, charismatic and activist voices throughout Black history. Because of both of the conditions listed above, institutions of Black Nationalism have been among the most vulnerable and simultaneously the most popular within the Black community.

Historically, the existence and development of Black Nationalistic institutions within the United States can best be described as periodic. Despite the fact that such institutions began developing in the 1840s, such institutions have not approached the numbers, specificity or variety found within the Black jeremiad. Black Nationalistic institutions remain broad based, and it appears that at least on the national level only one major institution per period has ever developed and been supported by the Black community.

Black Nationalistic institutions have, more than our other two traditions, been founded and/or led by activists and charismatic figures. As a result, the development and community support of these institutions has been sporadic—decades of intense activity followed by decades of quiescence. This has added to the marginal existence of these institutions. So too has the mystery surrounding the lives and deaths of Black Nationalistic leaders.

Still such institutions have survived, and at particular periods have drawn intense and widespread support from the community. This can be attributed to their institutional strategies and goals as much as, if not more than, to charisma. The goal of Black Nationalistic institutions has remained the same for more than two centuries—the political autonomy of Black people. The strategy through which that goal is pursued has been a severe critique of America as an Anglo American–dominated nation and an equally severe critique of Black people as a former slave population still lax in fully removing the shackles and developing political consciousness.

Black Cultural Pluralism

At this moment it is worth remembering both Cruse's and Kelley's admonitions that Black leaders have failed to properly prioritize Black culture in their formulations of the political. That is probably true, because institutions that have promoted

Black cultural pluralism within the United States are few and far between. These institutions have arisen primarily on the local level and not been thought of, at least previously, within a larger political context. The other fact is that the primary institutions of Black cultural pluralism are institutions peculiarly appropriate to narratives and the hidden transcript.[63] The truth is there are very few institutional avenues within the Black community, within the area of politics, for leadership to develop within this third tradition. And because other avenues are available within the other traditions, cultural pluralists have found it distinctly less difficult to further their goals within institutions of the other two traditions. Black cultural pluralism has historically supported the political agendas of *both* of the other two traditions without fully (or sometimes even marginally) agreeing with them, simply because they envisioned an increase in political space through such support.

However, cultural pluralism has been developed, and maybe more importantly, has dispersed its political understandings on the national level through the one institution available—Black culture. Levine, in his analysis of the development of Black folktales, especially those concerned with tricksters, heroes, bad men and bandits, tales that are essential in developing understandings of excellence, virtue and justice, with minor variations are nearly universal throughout Black communities in the United States.[64] With the popularity of the recording industry, Black music and the discourse surrounding Black music (on every level—the streets, community, within the Black intelligentsia) became national and at particular moments, international. During the last few decades, there has been significant development on the local level of various groups that take a distinctly holistic approach to Black existence in the United States. By holistic, I mean that their political understandings have been influenced by diet, issues of consumerism, etc., along with more traditional Black understandings of politics. Also we find that with the greater acceptance within the Black community of Africa, African people, and things African, many institutions founded distinctly within the Black jeremiad have, due to pressure of their constituency, adapted to Black cultural pluralism, in part or whole. These institutions include national Black magazines, local Black newspapers and even some historically Black colleges and universities. Still, this is a broad panorama, and Black cultural pluralism lacks strong institutions concerned primarily with the development of political thought, politics and political leaders. This inhibits the development of the tradition beyond the transitional phase. The tradition has produced a severe critique of the politics of American culture, but has yet to produce on a systematic level an understanding of justice upon which to base concepts of achievement.

Fragmenting Black Political Morality

At this stage, we return to our primary question of stasis. We seek to understand how political stasis within the Black community develops. It seems prudent to posit that the following reasons have contributed in an essential way to the development of stasis in the Black community: the lack of strong mediating institutions to develop a discourse of leadership within the Black community; philosophical and political discourses that are too narrow in scope to move beyond class, gender and other similar types of divisions within the Black community; competing political and institutional visions between two Black political traditions—Black Nationalism and the Black jeremiad; and the emergence of a third Black political tradition, cultural pluralism. We will begin this portion of our inquiry with that which is most apparent in facilitating the development of stasis—the conflict between Black Nationalism and the Black jeremiad.

Divisive Voices

For the first and only time in public, Dr. Martin Luther King Jr. met Malcolm X in New York City in 1964. Both were on their way to different events and happened to be at that particular place at the same moment. During that moment, a photograph was taken of them standing together. This is the only time they met in public. The photograph inspired an inventive moment in Spike Lee's production of the movie *Malcolm X*, and is the center of the fictional work *The Meeting*, by Jeff Stetson. Imbedded in that photograph, and mentioned and speculated upon in the two works concerning the meeting of Malcolm X and King, is the hope of reconciliation and cooperation, at the time between Martin and Malcolm, and ever since between Black Nationalism and the Black jeremiad.

The problem is that the root of political stasis is grounded in the foundations and promoted in the institutional goals and strategies of those two traditions. We must remember that at the beginning of our inquiry we posited that Du Bois' double aims—"on the one hand to escape White contempt and on the other hand the attempt to dig for a poverty-stricken horde"—lay directly beneath the surface of the conflict between integration and Black Nationalism. The first concern, to escape White contempt, has been institutionalized over the last two hundred years through the Black jeremiad as integrationist thought and politics. Integrationists seek to cultivate an understanding of human excellence among Black people based upon principles and values that are cultivated and developed primarily through the development of Anglo American political thought and action. The second concern, to dig for a poverty-stricken horde, has been institutionalized over the last two hundred years through various forms of Black Nationalist political thought and action. Black Nationalists seek to uncover, define and articulate an understanding of human excellence based upon principles and values that retain the goal of developing political autonomy for the Black community in the United States. While the double consciousness was apparent during Du Bois' writing of *Souls of Black Folk*, it has, with the growth of these two traditions and the development of their respective institutions, developed, becoming more sophisticated, subtle, and entrenched.[1]

Given the historical development of the Black jeremiad and Black Nationalism, outlined in the previous chapters, one should readily perceive that these traditions and their respective discourses are competitive and potentially polarizing:

> One ever feels his twoness,—an American, a Negro; two souls, two thoughts, two unreconciled strivings; two warring ideals in one dark body, whose dogged strength alone keeps it from being torn asunder.[2]

While Du Bois speaks to polarization of the psyche of the Black individual, we want to center our inquiry on polarization within the Black collective. I must here admit that I originally conceived of these two traditions as competing ideologies within a more unified Black political morality. However, a historical analysis reveals their philosophical and experiential distinctiveness. They are not overaggressive exaggerations of a truer philosophical tradition; each exhibits its own distinct and long history of developing a systematic understanding of the nature of

Black existence and positing its principles and goals as moral imperatives within the Black community.

As a moral imperative, the Black jeremiad seeks to dominate and claim, as its exclusive ideological terrain, the discourse of Black achievement. Alternatively, Black Nationalism seeks to dominate and claim, as its exclusive ideological terrain, the discourse of Black resistance. I am not here suggesting that either tradition operates exclusively in only one aspect or another of Black political morality. I am suggesting that particular environmental constraints such as resources, U.S. government policy, societal norms and expectations, etc., act to keep each tradition as narrow in scope as possible. These particular constraints, including the needs of the Black community, and the particular principles, values and goals of each tradition, are a large factor in each tradition fulfilling its specific function within the community. In their respective functions to uplift the Black community, they not only attempt to dominate certain areas of political morality, but in their competition for resources have focused their activities on particular sites within the community. These contested sites, most notably urban inner streets, Black churches and Black academia, have within the competing discourses become fragmented along the lines of gender, class, definitions and experiences of Blackness.

In fragmenting these sites, the respective traditions have proffered within them two competing visions of excellence. These visions operate on opposite ends of the spectrum. One requires members of the community to envision their development through the eventual dissolution of the community and movement into liberal American society. It is a vision oriented toward individual achievement and away from collective resistance. Excellence is perceived as finding one's niche within capitalistic society and contributing to the development of that society. The other requires members of the community to promote to the greatest degree possible autonomy of the community. It is a vision mired in collective resistance, while its expressed goal is collective achievement, although that goal has only been articulated in general terms. Excellence is perceived as opposing the exploitation of Anglo American capitalistic society and, in the moments when opposition is not required, developing the foundation of Black achievement.

Polarization of the community and eventual stasis within the community results as these two competing visions consume the resources of the community. In actuality most members of the Black community do not exist at the extreme of either vision, instead they transit between extremes and have some access to both visions. The stasis results from the individuals who do exist at the extremes and the resultant lack of leadership of individuals existing between poles. The individuals who do exist at the extremes are those most active in each tradition. These individuals in their activism usually center their existence within significant nation-oriented institutions of each respective tradition—the very same institutions that seek community resources and attempt to influence the political direction of the community. These activists usually come from the elite in both respective traditions. The current jeremiad elite includes individuals such as U.S. Supreme Court Justice Clarence Thomas, University of California Regent Ward Connerly, and Secretary of State Condoleezza Rice (and during Bush's first term, her predecessor, Colin Powell). Academics within this tradition include Thomas Sowell, Shelby Steele, and arguably Cornell West. The elite of Black Nationalism are strikingly different from those of the jeremiad, beginning with the most notable individual, Minister Louis Farrakhan. Black Nationalism elite normally develop within different parts of American society and the Black community. They choose or are forced into different educational paths than jeremiad elite, and obviously their professional careers are within often oppositional parts of American society and/or the Black community. While this is not always true, especially in regard to academics, the point being made is simply that their positions are often opposing and that their very active nature along with institutional opposition is the primary source of polarization and stasis in the Black community.

While these activists hold prominent positions in institutions both within and outside of the Black community, and while these institutions operate on local, national and international levels, we are here concerned mostly with the conflict within the Black community. We do have occasion to move beyond the community in our analysis of conflict, but only as it has significant influence within the community.

Blacks in Urban America

Historically, the Black jeremiad defines the streets of urban America as the site of rough, immoral, nihilistic, Black masculinity:

> Black people have always been in America's wilderness in search of a promised land. Yet many black folk now reside in a jungle ruled by a cutthroat market devoid of any faith in deliverance or hope for freedom. . . . What has led to the weakening of black cultural institutions in asphalt jungles?[3]

Urban streets are not particularly subject to institutional organization. Collectives that cannot be constrained by authoritative institutions pose a particular threat in any regime favoring order over freedom. One way to mitigate the threat is to stigmatize the threat. Urban streets have been stigmatized within Western literature for well over three centuries. In fact, the foundation of such an argument lies in Europe's medieval period and Christian philosophy. Beginning with Enlightenment literature, Europe has considered urban areas to be site of potential unhealthiness, both physically and morally. Due to that depiction, whether we consider it true or not, individuals within urban areas have always been subject to tighter governmental constraints. The Black jeremiad picked up on and developed that stigmatization and applied it to Black urban populations, especially Black males, with little reflection. West's argument that market forces—corporate market institutions—and insufficient Black leadership have broken down the barriers that once existed against nihilistic behavior is the most recent Black jeremiad variation among many Christian critiques of inner-city working-class people. The truth is that market forces drove modern European slavery, turned it into a continent-versus-continent phenomenon, and has since driven the maintenance of a racial and economic hierarchy that positions Black people and Black communities in particularly detrimental positions. Contrary to what West asserts, this is not a new phenomenon; America has always been a cutthroat jungle when race, economics and politics are meshed.

The work of UNIA, the Nation of Islam and later the Black Panthers, especially through the intellect, charisma and life example of Garvey and Malcolm, and the youthful energy and boldness of individuals such as Stokely Carmichael, Huey Newton, H. Rap Brown, etc., redeemed the black inner-city population and reconstructed the site as sympathetic to Black Nationalism and Black masculinity. The riots that burned throughout the United States over the last three decades solidified the streets as a site of Black masculinity, in fact, one of resistive Black masculinity.[4] The recent Million Man March was conceived by the Nation of Islam as a continuation, with slight variation, of this theme.

The Black jeremiad as a tradition with an ideology of integration has found little support within Black urban areas as a result of these two historical circumstances. It is in some manner a deserved suffering; however, that is not the point. The point is that lack of insight into urban Black culture—the unexamined acceptance of Western thought—has resulted in an ironic stigmatization for Black integrationists, especially males, by the Black working class. Because of this stigma, integrationists have moved further out of the Black community. That movement has been both physical and philosophical:

> What became clear to me is that people like myself, my friend, and middle-class blacks in general are caught in a very specific double bind that keeps two equally powerful elements of our identity at odds with each other. The middle-class values by which we were raised— the work ethic, the importance of education, the value of property ownership, of respectability, of "getting ahead," of stable family life, of initiative, of self-reliance, et cetera—are, in themselves, raceless and even assimilationist. . . . But the particular pattern of racial identification that emerged in the sixties and that still prevails today urges middle-class blacks (and all blacks) in the opposite direction. This pattern asks us to see ourselves as an embattled minority, and it urges an adversarial stance toward the mainstream and an emphasis on ethnic consciousness over individualism. It is organized around an implied separatism.[5]

Steele's grounding in the Black jeremiad causes him to classify opposition to Anglo American society as an ethos of victimization, and to see ambition and most other virtues (even those unnamed) as assimilationist values. Steele's work, which won the National Book Critics Circle Award in 1991, posits two faulty dichotomies that should raise immediate warning signs. First, it dichotomizes Black communities between assimilation and separatism. Second, it dichotomizes by assigning most positive virtues to assimilation and mires black working-class culture in the category of victimization—without virtue. Because Steele is so mired in the jeremiad tradition, which portrays suffering as essential, his snapshots of Black working-class culture reveal exactly this reliance on suffering. The twist that Steele and other jeremiad commentators apply to Black working-class culture is that unlike those in the middle class and middle-class aspirant, working-class Blacks only complain about suffering but fail to advance beyond. His vision of Black working-class culture is that it does not have the energy to do much beyond complaining. Interestingly, Steele's work still envisions adherents of the jeremiad, himself, and other middle-class blacks in general, as victims of a double bind.

Steele's apology for Black middle-class individualism is indicative of the fact that due to their view of Black culture, such individuals are much more willing to suffer to become part of the structure of the American hierarchy. Steele is even willing to classify himself and all middle-class Blacks as victims of working-class Black ideology to reenergize the moral imperatives of the jeremiad. On the other hand, Steele exhibits no willingness to suffer for the development of Black culture, and if we take a long hard look at most post–Civil Rights movement integrationist works, they no longer exhibit as a core theme the imperative of uplifting the race. It has since been subsumed by elite individualism. Within his own dichotomy, Steele embraces assimilation as excellence. Steele's attempt to construct simplistic dichotomies to explain his identity crisis in political terms cannot obscure the greater complexity of Black existence. The stark naked truth is that what Steele defines as implied separatism could consist of anything from cultural pluralism to political separatism. The conclusion that it is implied separatism is simply due to the ongoing conflict with Black Nationalism, a historical reluctance to envision the self-determination of Black culture and an ignorance of the resultant emergence of Black cultural pluralism as a third Black tradition.

Competition between jeremiad and Nationalist agendas also affects the vitality of Black spiritualism. Black spiritualism underwent significant development during the height of the integration/Nationalist conflict. That development changed the way that Blacks, especially young urban Blacks, perceive Black churches as *cultural* institutions.

On the one hand, Black Nationalist organizations attacked Black Christianity as a passive religion that was conducive to the development of slavery and oppression. This attack was led by Black socialists and Marxists who, within their philosophy, understood religion as a crutch of superstitious peoples who had come under control of capitalists:

> Echoing Karl Marx, V.F. Calverton charged in 1927 that religion was kind of "otherworldliness" among Blacks. The traditional Judeo-Christian ethic of forgiveness, submissive behavior, prayer for salvation and tolerance toward one's earthly oppressors simply perpetuated white racism and the brutal extraction of surplus value from the labor power of the Black proletariat.[6]

Younger Black Nationalists, such as Stokely Carmichael and Huey Newton, not only viewed the philosophical tenets of Black Christianity as problematic, but perceived the day-to-day strategy of the Black Christian–led Civil Rights movement as equally flawed.

> With the sudden renaissance of Black nationalism in the guise of Black Power, both King and his entire generation of activist-ministers received a profound jolt. SNCC activist Julius Lester's *Look Out Whitey! Black Power's Gon' Get Your Mama!* repeated Jones's denunciation of King as merely the "successor of Booker T. Washington." King's message of "love" was hypocritical, Lester declared.[7]

This attack against Black Christianity was echoed by the Nation of Islam, who deprecated Christianity as the White man's religion and at the time claimed the White man a creation of an evil experiment.

On the other hand, integrationists hoping to capitalize on the resurgence of the Black Church brought upon by the popularity of Dr. King among the Black working class attempted to use Black Christianity as legitimization for assimilation/integration ideologies:

> King articulated the Salvationist vision of a future but accessible utopia, a golden place whose every ethical and moral stone was familiar to this widely dispersed congregation. Baker and others, whose genius rested in organization and the analyses of social process, recognized both King's unquestioned authority and his obvious limitations. Baker was appalled by the other SCLC leaders' deference to and dependency on King. But they too were hedged in by the prescripted narrative of Black Salvationism. Thus while a Baker or an Abernathy or a Clark might provide organizational integument—that is, practical planning and realistic goals to King's paradigmatic talk—the power of the movement came from the masses. . . . in King they saw their own reflection. . . . thus Wilkins, in the cocoon of what Max Weber termed a bureaucratic institution, was (situationally and by habits of thought) unqualified to imagine or recognize the nature of the movement.[8]

What many integrationists failed to recognize is that Black Christianity formed only one essential element of Black culture and Black political morality. Maybe even more significant is the failure to understand that Black spirituality is in fact an essential foundation of Black cultural pluralism, more so than being a potential juncture of integration. It was partially due to this slight mistake that integrationists were seen as hypocritical and deprecated as opportunists. They viewed Black Christianity as a temporary tool of organizing the masses, while at the same time perceiving the tool almost in the same manner as Black Nationalists.

The attachment to the integrationist agenda and the historic animosity toward Black street life held by most Black Christian churches became a distinct problem during the 1960s. Following the death of Martin Luther King Jr., as the Civil Rights movement gave way to the Black Power movement, Black churches, which had historically stigmatized Black street life, found it hard to retain young members, especially young Black males:

> King and other Black ministers succeeded in their efforts to achieve democratic reforms within the capitalistic democratic system, but were unable to alleviate the sufferings of the Black masses caused by institutional racism and capitalism. As the Black Power and Vietnam War destroyed the fragile consensus among the petty bourgeois leadership of the Civil Rights Movement, King was pressured to move to the left. With the courage instilled by his nonviolent convictions, he advanced a progressive human rights agenda at home and abroad, and began to make the case for economic democracy. The majority of Black clergy were then, and still are today, unable to follow King's example established in 1966–1968.[9]

The Nation of Islam, due to both philosophic and strategic problems, has not fulfilled what initially appeared to be the potential to attract significant number of Black young people during the 1970s. Among the generation of Black males and females that reached the age of maturity in the '60s and '70s, many remain outside the influence of Black religious institutions.

Instead of developing Black spiritualism as a point of organization, integrationists and Nationalists alike tended to expose the vulnerability of adherents to Black spirituality. Those whose spirituality was strong became sacrifices to the cause, and those least spiritual profited. As those attempting to integrate lunch counters were beaten, as angry, righteous rioters were jailed, as individual leaders including Malcolm and Martin became martyrs, it became clear that the hierarchy being established within the Black community itself was one that exploited Black spiritualism, Black political morality and Black culture.

While it should not be mistaken that Black spiritualism was torn asunder by this conflict and exploitation, it should be noted that within our third tradition it did cause Black spiritualism to revert back to its previous hidden transcript and narrative forms, thus moving Black faith, an essential political virtue, outside of institutional influence. As a consequence, the Black community suffers. The essential aspect of that suffering is not the reduction of congregation size, but the inability to develop strong spiritual leadership that operates within Black institutions in the tradition of Malcolm and Martin. Young Black people have not perceived the Black church as the foundation of the community as did generations before them.

Turning to other avenues, they have left Black spiritualism with a glaring void. As remnants of the Civil Rights movement achieve retirement, those in Reverend Jesse Jackson's generation, Black spiritual leadership suffers further, especially on the national level. The same holds true in the area of Black Nationalism with the aging of Minister Louis Farrakhan.

Black spiritualism no longer finds itself in a position to mediate the debate between nationalists and integrationists. The dogged strength that Du Bois referred to as that which held together the two component parts of Black identity, at least on the collective level, has itself been polarized and subsequently constrained by Black jeremiad and Black Nationalist ideological and institutional conflict. The Black spiritual experience no longer motivates, circumscribes and/or constrains disparate Black political institutions. What is occurring within the discourse is the incremental devaluation of spiritualism as an essential element of strength within the Black community.

Intellectual Specialization

Historically, leadership within the Black community is broad based. While the model of broad-based Maroon leadership may not be feasible in contemporary Black culture, the need for leaders to facilitate amalgamation, adaptation, inclusiveness and improvisation remains essential to successful development. Modern commentators persistently speak of coalition building with groups outside of the Black community. However, such coalition building is most likely premature, and given the scope of current Black leadership, nearly impossible. While some barriers may be practical—economic and political mistrust and self-interest—Black leaders have rarely shown a propensity to build essential coalitions within the community. In the area of coalition building, neither the jeremiad nor Nationalism has successfully constructed and experienced coalition building within their respective discourses to create a prototype upon which Black leaders can draw.

Alternatively, Black leaders, including King and Malcolm, have become popular, as Robinson suggests of King, because the Black masses have seen in these individuals their own reflection. This was true of Toussaint, Dessalines, Washington and Garvey. We should not forget these same masses have also been willing to turn away from popular leaders when they betray that reflection. The more essential position of our current inquiry is that Black leaders achieve popularity within the Black community by being broad-based multidimensional individuals or by working (as King did) to achieve that broad-based multidimensional understanding. Levine's historical analysis of the complexity of Black political morality must be taken seriously. A community with such a level of complexity both politically and morally demands, has always demanded, broad-based multidimensional leadership.

The problem is that increasing specialization and the conflict between Black Nationalism and the Black jeremiad has increasingly narrowed the scope of understanding of Black leaders. As the contest over limited community resources heightens, institutional leaders concerned primarily with preservation of particular institutions tend to narrow their focus. For King's and Malcolm's generation it took circumstances, events and fortune to produce broad-based leadership. In other words, it was the leaders who moved to the position of the masses who earned the masses' attention—not the other way around. Leaders within jeremiad and Nationalistic institutions are currently incapable of such movement primarily due to institutional constraints—such institutions have begun to think of their institutional survival as synonymous with the survival of the Black community. Such a position is not only fallacious but dangerous. Since these institutions tend to lie on both sides of the conflict, they also have the tendency in promotion of this self-interest to polarize of the community. Unconstrained self-interest has the propensity to debilitate essential compromise. The lack of compromise debilitates the possibility of broad-based leadership—the scope of leadership narrows while the community it seeks to serve becomes more dynamic and multidimensional.

If the double consciousness remains the functional Black consciousness in this environment, then any attempted subversion of the double consciousness is detrimental—one essential source of divisiveness within the community. That both Nationalists and integrationists have attempted to subvert Black consciousness for their own interests is evident:

> The opposing thrust of these two parts of our identity results in the double bind of middle-class blacks. There is no forward movement on either plane that does not constitute backward movement on the other. This was the familiar trap I felt myself in while talking with my friend. As I spoke about class, his eyes reminded me that I was betraying my race. Clearly, the two indispensable parts of my identity were a threat to one another.[10]

For Steele and other integrationists, the subversion is graphic. Against all historical evidence, they choose to believe that Black culture cultivates and develops no redeeming qualities, that it is irrationally oppositional toward Anglo American culture and therefore disastrous. All of the values that they have seen as profitable, even though they recognize some of these values as universal, they refuse to situate in Black culture. Black culture is only reconstructed as a reaction to Anglo America. For integrationists, even though Black culture exists in opposition, it is passive, reactionary. Integrationists derogate Black culture and Black consciousness purely to the area of resistance. Beyond resistance, it has no value. Such a position posits that there is no such thing—since Steele cannot situate any positive values in Black culture—as Black achievement. So to achieve, integrationists such as Steele confine and constrain themselves within Anglo American culture. Like most

Anglo Americans, most integrationists perceive Black culture as detrimental to *true* achievement. Unlike most Anglo Americans, they understand Black culture and Black resistance almost entirely as a Black Nationalist discourse—a discourse they will engage in only if their existence is threatened. This all but precludes any type of compromise with Black Nationalists. Maybe more importantly it tends to derogate most of Black life.

> Beloved leaders and guides of the people, when we say "polluted in the blood," it means we still live the life of a slave. We don't think like free men. We go to the capitals of America and Europe, like paupers, weak, to demand or ask for what unjust regimes will never give. Unless we develop power to force unjust governments to yield to our just demands, then we will never achieve what we desire for our people. All French-speaking countries are tied to France and the blood of old colonialism is covering all Francophone leaders. All Anglophone leaders are tied to England. All of us are tied to our former masters in one way or another and, therefore, we don't talk about real freedom, we talk about emancipation. But what is the true meaning of the word? Emancipation does not mean freedom. Emancipation comes from the Latin word "mancipere," which means, "to free from your hand but not from your control." You are free from the hand of Europe, but you are still under the control of Europe. We are free from the hand of the government of America, but we are still tied to them in many other ways. Until we can truly cut the umbilical cord and come to a state of real independence, we are fooling ourselves.[11]

The strange twist, the irony of modern Black Nationalist discourse such as the statement of Minister Louis Farrakhan immediately above, is that it also derogates Black culture in an attempt to redeem Black power. Not unlike integrationists, Nationalists perceive Black culture as weak, immature, effeminate and ineffectual—slave culture. Nationalists, such as Farrakhan, develop this ironic critique through the same misreading of Black history as integrationists. The one glaring difference is that Nationalists believe in Black achievement—believe that it is the ultimate goal, especially in terms of Black power. In fact, without Black achievement they believe, as Farrakhan's address to African heads of state indicates, that Blacks exist as slaves. Obviously this position, which classifies integrationists as slaves, offers no points of compromise to adherents of the Black jeremiad. Maybe more importantly, it, like the jeremiad position, derogates the culture and consciousness of most Black people.

The Black Nationalist position precludes the double consciousness in the terms that it was formulated by Du Bois and in the context by which it is experienced by Blacks in the United States and other areas of the Diaspora. The Nationalistic argument cannot be belittled or critiqued by default—it is a powerful and insightful argument *when treated philosophically*. If one side of an identity must be dominant, then that dominance is not only determined by inner strength, whether individual or collective, it is also determined by environment. In fact, the real philosophical question that Black Nationalists pose is whether or not a consciousness that faces essential external constrains can be understood and developed as a true separate and unique consciousness.

The problem with the Black Nationalistic critique is that it exists much like the integrationist critique of Black culture as a false dichotomy. Again we need refer back to Levine's articulation of a complex Black consciousness to understand why such a simple dichotomy is disastrous. Black leadership promoting such a simple dichotomy will always find lukewarm response to their message and also perceive such messengers as only being peripherally attached to Black culture—never understanding its weaknesses and strengths. In such a leader most Black people cannot envision themselves, unless that leader brings with him that Black cultural experience, including the vulnerability, that Malcolm X brought to Nationalism. If envisioning self in one's leadership is impossible, then it is equally impossible to envision the strength required to pull together the component parts of the Black community. By refusing to reconstruct and develop that which Du Bois understood as soul force, "dogged strength," that which keeps the disparate components of the double consciousness from ripping asunder Black consciousness, adherents of the Black jeremiad and Black Nationalism tend to subvert such strength, deprecating it as weakness, and severely debilitating its development.

Specialization tends to undercut the development of broad-based leadership. By undercutting this historical strength of Black leadership, competing traditions have confiscated from themselves and the Black community essential components (leadership and discourse) of developing politics and philosophy. By imposing noncultural models of politics and philosophy upon the Black community, they make it very difficult to develop a discourse that facilitates coalition building and compromise between fundamental factions within the community.

The truth of Nationalism and the jeremiad is that while they are distinct traditions, their strategies within the American context have led most commentators to articulate them as ideologies.[12] Laying claims to disparate sites of resistance and achievement within the Black community only exacerbates such faulty articulations. Even as these two traditions have fought for their own legitimacy within the American context, both have failed to recognize Black cultural pluralism as a legitimate tradition within that same context. Most often they have failed to recognize the strength of Black culture as a legitimate, self-determinant discourse within the American context. In this regard, both traditions develop institutions that, in regard to the Black community, employ the primary methodology of evangelizing. This has also led to their competition, as their primary method of uplifting the race has been lifting individuals into the privileges of Anglo American culture or uplifting Black culture itself by realigning Black priorities. In this methodology of conversion, both the jeremiad and Nationalism have met with extremely limited success. Despite limited success, they have done little to change their respective methodologies, which further mires the community in stasis.

Due to their narrow, often deprecating methodologies, these institutions and individuals can rarely understand and articulate the breadth and complexity of the political and moral experience of the Black community. In fact the integration/Nationalism dichotomy more correctly characterizes *competition among elite Black political and economic institutions for Black mass patronage.* The immediate problem is not that these organizations and institutions do not have what they believe to be the best interests of the Black community in mind. In fact, they may indeed have such interests in mind and attempt to synthesize them within their institutional agendas. We may even go so far as to vigorously argue that most organizational and institutional agendas are, or at least once were, directly derived from Black mass interests. Still, the problem remains in the daily interpretation of these interests into a general political paradigm, political morality and/or political theory. Such interpretations must take place at the level of culture to be successful.

Static Voices

The integration/Nationalism dichotomy does not and cannot properly reflect the political history of the Black community. One distinct reason this is true is because of our third tradition. Black cultural pluralism maintains as rich a tradition as the Black jeremiad and Nationalism. Maintaining that tradition through narratives and hidden transcripts, it has created strong cultural institutions within the United States. The primary reason for the development of narratives and hidden transcripts has been the paucity of institutions with the ability to further the political agenda of cultural pluralism. In resistance it aligns itself with both the jeremiad and Black Nationalism and has consistently committed resources to both while consistently critiquing both traditions. Cultural pluralists have also consistently shied away from both traditions to the extent that they have deprecated Black culture. In achievement, cultural pluralists retain a fragile alliance with Black Nationalism and the jeremiad. Still, the constraints of both traditions as currently formulated do not and cannot reach the Black cultural pluralists on the cultural level—the level of existence.

Within most major Black cultural institutions—the family, and various community-based institutions, especially Black music—Nationalism and integration have been significantly constrained by more immediate experiences of achievement and resistance as articulated in discourses of Black cultural pluralism. In the more stable of these institutions, it appears that individuals and small groups strike a balance between achievement and resistance. The same appears to be true within Anglo American institutions in which large numbers of Blacks participate, such as professional sports and the military. In fact, it appears that Black people treat achievement and resistance as mutually cooperative components, using each to promote the other and both to advance cultural development.

Therein rests the moral and political dilemma: Exactly because the existential necessities of Black communities are much more dynamic, defined more broadly, than either of the methodologies and goals of our two most institutionally active traditions allow, these necessities cannot be precisely articulated by existing Black institutions or even broader political movements.[13] For example, even though Black mass resistance has received some form of legitimization in the last 30 years, because of organizational priorities, that sanction has been particularly aimed at Black masculinity and has made Black resistance a particularly masculine venue within the Nationalism/integrationist dichotomy. In fact, Rosa Parks' quiet, exhausted anger was sculpted to fit within the scope of proper femininity, integration and the jeremiad. What, however, become of the Eula Loves and Latasha Harlins, whose anger at an oppressive system erupts much more spontaneously, graphically and much further beyond the boundaries of traditional understandings? The organizational and ideological concerns poised to make opportunity of one are badly situated to adequately develop the others—in the case of both Nationalism and the jeremiad.

Consequently, the eruption of Black cultural pluralism and the anger of our Cincinnati youth—only Black cultural pluralism as a distinct tradition could aggregate sufficient energy required to demand that their voice be heard beyond the Black community. The constraint that Black cultural pluralism has yet to move beyond is the fact that it remains in a transitional state between achievement and resistance—which makes its responses appear spontaneous. In this sense, it is static. The static nature of the environment obviously creates a sense of anxiety and frustration. Human nature demands development beyond the state of resistance.

Recognizing this, the voice of our Cincinnati youth should resonate even more deeply. The sacrifices necessary to build essential political institutions and philosophical discourses within this third tradition have been too few and far between. Black culture, often compromised before the 1960s by arguments of inferiority, in the post–1960s is too often compromised by money and reputation to engage in institution and discourse development. Our third tradition, and by extension the Black community, continues to suffer from a dearth of institutions, most notably viable political institutions, that can deal with the crisis of stasis on the cultural level.

Institutional Development

In the sense that Nationalism and the jeremiad have both developed methodologies more conducive to evangelism than developing bridges between conflicting interests, the institutions within these two traditions are more conducive to acquiring resources as opposed to facilitating compromise and cooperation within the community. At the moment of this writing, I would argue that there exists no significant institutions within the Black community that operate on the national level with the goal of facilitating compromise and cooperation within the community. I would further argue there also exists no significant discourse in Black political thought with this goal. Finally I will posit that since the decline of the Civil Rights movement, the creation and development of such institutions have been essential to the development of the Black community on both the political and cultural level.

The immediate problem is that due to the development of the jeremiad and Nationalistic traditions, creation of such institutions remains outside of their particular constraints. Instead of viewing Black culture as a site of political conflict, they view it as a sight of moral deficiency and ignore legitimate conflicts in their goal of impressing upon Black culture their particular moral hierarchy. Their ability to hear Black voices outside of their particular constraints is extremely limited. Consequently, both traditions continue to evangelize, perceiving the lack of interest in establishing either moral hierarchy as endemic to contemporary Black culture. On the other hand, Black cultural pluralists have demonstrated a particular lack of excellence in developing institutions in an area in which they are particularly historically situated.

I make this argument based on Du Bois' allusion to dogged strength. I believe that dogged strength is indeed cultural in its derivation. In fact, I believe that it is the foundation of Black culture—Black spiritualism. Other traditions because of their deprecation of Black culture have little access beyond intuition to this strength. This lack of access and understanding abounds in their discourse and their institutional agendas.

This lack of mediating institutions has had an adverse affect on leadership in the community. Black political leaders are primarily trained in either the Nationalistic or jeremiad tradition. This incrementally moves them outside of Black culture, in regards to political thought and action. Interests become more fragmented within various traditions and within various understandings of particular traditions. Leaders are developed in dichotomous evangelic traditions that envision excellence as strict adherence to one side of the dichotomy and view adherence to the other side as moral and political deficiency. Without strong institutions to mediate, the problem has a circular effect, and proliferates.

Healing Black Political Morality

The question of culture obviously is essential to answering our questions of Black political morality. If we consider culture as an essential foundation of existence, such arguments and traditions that question the existence and/or purpose of Black culture *ultimately question the validity of Black existence*. In the introduction to his edition on Black philosophy, *Existence in Black*, Lewis Gordon takes exactly this route. Gordon considers the question of "Why Blacks go on living under the conditions they do" to be one of the primary philosophical concerns of European and European American scholars when dealing with the Black community.[1] Even though Gordon reaffirms Black existence in relation to this question, one wonders why, with more than 40 million Black people in the United States, not to mention billions of Blacks throughout the rest of the Diaspora and Africa, he considers this question so essential that it should frame the discourse within Black philosophy? We have proved that our existence is essential, at least to ourselves. The real question is not why, but how Blacks should live. To answer that question, we move to the question of bridging gaps, developing traditions and creating a favorable balance in the Black community between resistance and achievement.

Creative Voices

A reading of the thinkers included in this anthology suggests an initial characterization of philosophy within this tradition as essentially an intellectual power of *mediation*. It is the philosopher's role, for example, to mediate the desires and expectations of the individual with the interests of the collective, interests that the philosopher will be quick to acknowledge are themselves largely responsible for the particular contour of the individual's desires and expectations. [2]

The quote above can be found in the introductory essay of *I Am Because We Are*, an anthology of Black Philosophy. Hord and Lee posit a radical argument: that Black political philosophy assumes a role of conflict resolution between competing understandings:

> Philosophy can play the role of mediator that we have outlined precisely because it is at its best a discipline sensitive to the values of both universality and cultural particularity. . . . Philosophy—again, at its best—is able to uncover, articulate, and nurture precisely those aspects of a particular cultural tradition that seem best suited to universalization for the purpose of building bridges between various distinct cultural traditions. [3]

We should begin with the last part of Hord and Lee's argument—the idea that the role of the philosopher is to effect bridges between cultural traditions. It is a task that outlines a future for Black philosophy. [4] To a great extent, the future that Hord and Lee outline is a future that is not immediately functional. The reason that it is not immediately functional is because Black philosophers have not yet adequately understood Black culture, politics and philosophy. We have yet to understand the development of separate philosophical traditions within the Black community. Maybe more essential, too, many political and moral chasms remain within the community itself that beg our attention. Concerning these chasms, Black philosophers have gained very little experience in building bridges. In other words, Black philosophers need to first gain experience building bridges *within* the Black cultural tradition before we begin to look without. This initial step is essential to Black development. This initial step is the initial requirement of developing Black political thought and action beyond stasis.

The key to building bridges within the Black community lies in Du Bois' allusion to dogged strength. Any discourse that seeks to mediate conflicts within the Black community must be developed at the cultural level. In that context, Black cultural pluralism exhibits the most promising development despite its paucity of institutions. Cultural pluralism has on the practical level an intimate knowledge of both the jeremiad and Nationalism. This level of knowledge is essential to mediating such a historical conflict. Maybe more essential is that cultural pluralism speaks and hears voices within the same context of our Cincinnati youth—it communicates on that level without exploitation.

Black Spiritualism

Perhaps, the most daunting task is that of reenergizing Black spiritualism and reconstructing it as a political resource within the community, especially a resource for Black youth. Setting aside commentators such as West, who accuse inner-city Black youth of nihilism, the truth is Black youth have retained their spiritualism— it is we who are searching. What I mean, more precisely, is that just as generations of Black youth have developed their spiritualism within the context of Black music, so too has the present generation. Kelley alone among major Black thinkers recognizes the extent of this experience in the last chapter, "Kickin' Reality, Kickin' Ballistics," of *Race Rebels*. While Kelley does not reconstruct the music of Black youth as a medium for the development of spiritualism—the elements of such a reconstruction are there.

As Black youth moved beyond the confines of integration and a Black Christianity steeped in promoting integration at any cost, lacking sufficient trust in Islam, spiritualism for many became an activity that could no longer sufficiently develop within the constraints of traditional religious institutions. Youth found a more complete faith in music that promoted an unrelenting truth:

> In other words, Nigga is not merely *another* word for black. Products of the postindustrial ghetto, the characters in gangsta rap constantly remind listeners that they are still second-class citizens—"Niggaz"—whose collective experiences suggest that nothing has changed *for them*. . . . Their point is simple: the experiences of young black men in the inner city are not universal to all black people, and, in fact, they recognize that some African Americans play a role in perpetuating their oppression. . . . By linking their identity to the "hood" instead of simply skin color, gangsta rappers implicitly acknowledge the limitations of racial politics, including black middle-class reformism as well as black nationalism.[5]

While Kelley understands the music of Black youth in political terms, we also need to be aware of the moral implications. One can clearly hear the voice of faith developing through music and in the culture that surrounds the music; more than anything, the faith centers upon the experience of what many contemporary youth pronounce as "keeping it real." This experience not only defines the context out of which faith is constructed, it defines the parameters and goals of Black faith. Steeped in a context of opposing exploitation, it centers faith in the community by heightening individual consciousness. Obviously, it requires individuals within the community to transition beyond the rewards in the afterlife and focus upon the immediate context. Less obviously, it reconstructs a pantheon of Black morality grounded in a particular understanding of reality. Black youth, rappers and artists in other genres such as hip hop, gospel and R&B do not suggest that reality is utopian; instead they center reality in their harsh environment, so harsh, in fact, they often find themselves corrupted. They do not in anyway suggest it is something that they can overcome; they only suggest that it is something they must overcome.

An interesting aspect of the music of Black youth, indeed a historical aspect of Black music in general, is its ability to transit with little difficulty beyond otherwise formidable borders of race, class and culture. Here I am not speaking of the phenomenon of crossover music, but instead I am speaking of the popularity of Black music—from inner-city gangsta rap to contemporary gospel to contemporary R&B—among contemporary youth. The truth is, Black music does not need to transform itself to appeal to Anglo American youth. The point I want to focus on is within the Black community. Recording artists have historically cultivated the ability to articulate complex experiences across difficult barriers; contemporary Black youth continues to develop within that tradition. Within the Black community, music has demonstrated its ability to "uncover, articulate, and nurture precisely those aspects of the Black cultural tradition that seem best suited to universalization."[6] It also retains the potential to act as an institution of mediation, "building bridges between various distinct cultural traditions."[7] I bring this up to point out definitively that universalization within Black culture can be achieved, in fact is being achieved on a particular level through a historically essential medium. Outside of "traditional" moral institutions, then, Black spiritualism thrives, universalizing moral understandings within the Black community—universalizing without destroying the uniqueness or vitality of any of our three traditions or the youth seeking their spiritualism.

Cultural pluralists, then, must develop institutions that can cultivate and protect such spiritual energy. Current institutions have failed, at least in the last function. Yet to develop spiritual institutions, the Black community must move beyond the Nationalist/integrationist discourse and the constraints of traditional religious institutions. I have occasion to experience strong Black spiritualism in a variety of venues, including Black poetry readings, Black rallys, Black graduations, the Martin Luther King Day Parade down King Boulevard in Los Angeles, etc. I have experienced the catharsis of Black spiritualism on the faces of youth at each of these events, observed youth deep in spiritual thought. Each of these events has promoted Black culture, but each has also promoted cultural pluralism. I have also noticed that such events promote Black spiritualism through amalgamation, each without proselytizing, each without constraining particular understandings, each without symbols of nation and state. What is dominantly being promoted and where the spiritualism lies is the most fundamental element in any society—people.

One aspect left unmentioned is class. The truth is, each of these events is minimally tied to the class phenomenon that continues to develop within Black culture and threatens all systems of achievement. Still, these events are driven to a large extent by the Black historical memory, as is the medium (Black music), which serves as their foundation. Most Black people understand the problems incurred by the Black church due to its deprecating of working-class Black culture. There is an attempt to amalgamate the phenomenon of class through these events. The fact is, many of these events develop out of Black working culture; the struggle is to keep their original meaning and their continued development within the community. One thing that the rap explosion has taught us is that all levels of community are equally corruptible and even a seemingly straightforward faith such as "keeping it real" becomes complex within the context of American capitalism.

That which is lacking is a discourse within the community concerning Black spiritualism. The discourses that claim to concern Black spiritualism are jeremiad derivatives that seek to revive Black Christianity, most often by deprecating other components of the Black community, especially working-class Black people. As an aside, this is a most interesting and depressing phenomenon—a religious institution that historically acts in a derogatory manner toward the very section it relies on for much of its constituency. The problem is this discourse cannot divorce itself from the Anglo American tradition of evangelism among the natives. Nor can this discourse divorce itself from its conflict with Nationalism; for both traditions, evangelism remains essential.

Cultural pluralism can develop a discourse beyond evangelism through amalgamation. To achieve this we must only understand the depths of Black spiritualism and listen to all voices within these depths. Such is our task:

> . . . and the spiritual striving of the freedmen's sons is the travail of souls whose burden is almost beyond the measure of their strength, but who bear it in the name of an historic race, in the name of this land of their fathers' fathers, and in the name of human opportunity.[8]

Balancing Achievement and Resistance

This leads us to the second task, that of developing a functional balance between resistance and achievement. No understanding of politics can be so designed as to prevent people from hearing voices of resistance. Thomas Jefferson understood this in his call for a constitution of government that allowed the possibility of revolution within the context of government each generation. Jefferson was summarily ignored. Currently in the United States there exists very little balance between resistance and achievement. Consequently it has taken more than two hundred years since the first state prohibited slavery for Blacks to receive acceptance as equal citizens within the American context. The political context that exists in the United States gears American institutions toward keeping order and control; the resistive voice represents a disruptive voice. In an attempt to maintain order, the resistive voice if it is not destroyed is channeled through institutions geared toward "civilizing" resistance so that it accepts its place in the order. This Black people should intuitively understand. In paradigms that stress hierarchy, this is both unavoidable and understandable. To truly allow resistive voice would indeed by laudable. To achieve this allowance, institutions must be historically aware. Such is not the case in the United States. As a nation, the United States shuns history and especially the history reconstructed by resistive voices. History interferes with order. The problem for America is that democracy demands resistance.

Black institutions and leaders must develop the courage American institutions lack, the courage to consult history and to violate the sanctity of order. Again we return to Du Bois' allusion of dogged strength. We envisioned this dogged strength as both amalgamation and improvisation in Maroon communities through a methodology that made it possible for leaders to bring into the community a variety of spiritual concerns and within that variety create and develop a "loas" that provided *political* focus to the community. In the post-emancipation era, an essential example of such dogged strength in the context of balancing resistance and achievement became apparent in the life example of Martin Luther King Jr. King, in his pursuit of Civil Rights, integrating individual Blacks within the American political system, surprisingly heard voices, collective voices, that most people believed he should not have heard. These voices came from Black youth and their disenchantment with the Vietnam War, and individuals economically impoverished whose voices eventually led him to Memphis. These voices also led him beyond the constraints of his tradition, the Black jeremiad. The jeremiad vision was focused on achievement at the moment and perceived working-class resistance as a disruptive influence within such a context. King understood that some balance within the Black community was required between achievement and resistance. King's ability to hear, understand and then articulate these voices within the context of the Black community and mainstream America was one of the most potent displays of political mediation achieved within the modern context.

Such strength is necessary to reconcile resistance and achievement and find them of equal value in political thought and action. Once again we find cultural pluralism uniquely and historically situated to understand and develop such understandings of human excellence. The question of institutionalization persists. I can only point in this case to Black grassroots organizations (maybe more properly called collectives), which have attempted to develop a holistic philosophy that includes health and environment as part of the political terrain. Still, the fact that the Black community remains dynamic and resistive in relation to hierarchical systems is also encouraging.

Developing a Systematic Understanding of Justice

The next task is to develop a systematic understanding of justice based upon this balance. Justice is ultimately the destination of any sound discourse of political thought and action. It is the destination of our inquiry. At this point, Black political thought has yet to develop a systematic understanding of justice beyond resistance. Critiques of justice, which have been proffered by the Black jeremiad and

Black Nationalism, are forms of resistance. The Black community has developed intense critiques to most current forms of justice. What most of these critiques exhibit is the historical development in thought and action of Black unwillingness to accept and more essentially perpetuate understandings and systems of exploitation. This unwillingness appears vague, but it comes through in the commitment to community and the continued willingness to promote community above and beyond American articulations of individuality. This promotion of community is demonstrated on the basic level of politics and economics. It is interesting because of the mass support it has received and the tradition that has historically promoted it as a core component of Black political thought and action. The first example of such mass support we reconstructed through the Haitian constitution, which granted full citizenship status to Europeans who fought with the Haitian rebels for independence, and through the adoption of the national name Haiti, a derivative of *Ayti*, the name given the island by the Arawak, the indigenous inhabitants of the island. The second example was through Garvey's critique of "bombastic negroes," whom he warned against returning to Africa for the purposes of exploiting. The fact that these acts were centered upon events in which the actors were primarily concerned with the acquisition of Black power and are now centered in a discourse similarly situated, identifies them as core values, strong core values.

This is the foundation where any systematic understanding of justice in the Black community must begin. Unlike our previous categories, I believe that all three traditions are historically situated to contribute to such a discourse. All three traditions have in different circumstances exhibited and sustained an abhorrence of exploitation. The problem for the Black jeremiad has been the inability to overcome the reliance upon the American jeremiad. Neither has Black Nationalism gone beyond focusing its critique of justice upon Anglo American institutions and Black culture. Consequently, a discourse attempting to develop understandings of justice must begin with mediation within the context of Black culture; it is out of that mediation that clearer patterns of justice will begin to emerge and be defined within the Black community.

One of the most profound texts to come out of the inner-city context in the post–Civil Rights era is the work of Sanyika Shakur (Kody Scott), *Monster*. While *Monster* is formally written as the autobiography of a Los Angeles gang member, the contested terrain in the work centers around Shakur's developing understanding of community. This understanding allows him to progress from frightened individual to gang member to Black Nationalist whose concerns for his community land him once again in prison, and finally to an author whose text demonstrates under the worst conditions the Black commitment to community:

> And what about the children? What do we tell them, or our wives? How do we come to grips with the fact that this thing has gotten way too real, out of control like some huge snow-

ball rolling down a hill, threatening to smash and kill all in its path, including those who originally fashioned it . . . the children deserve to have a decent childhood where they live. They shouldn't have to be uprooted to the suburbs to experience peace. We cannot contaminate them with our feuds of madness, which are predicated on factors over which we have no control.[9]

This level of commitment to community under the most adverse conditions has given me pause to consider, in the context of *Monster*, the following statement:

> To understand the significance of internal conflict among African Americans, we need to examine how communities are constructed and sustained rather than begin with the presumption that a tight-knit, harmonious black community has always existed (until recently) across time and space. This sort of romantic view of a "golden age" of black community—an age when any elder could beat a misbehaving child, when the black middle class mingled with the poor and offered themselves as "role models," when black professionals cared more about their downtrodden race than their bank accounts—is not only disingenuous but has stood in the place of serious historical research on class relations within African American communities.[10]

While Kelley may be correct in demanding a level of analysis that looks beyond the romanticism of the golden age, as we have looked beyond that romanticism to the fundamental construction and development of most Black communities, we have found the essential importance of amalgamation within those communities that have endured. One aspect of *Monster* that most people find disconcerting is the division ripe within inner-city communities. Street versus street, neighborhood versus neighborhood. The fact is, the degree of fragmentation is astounding exactly in the sense that most who are into gang activity are impoverished and hold in common a variety of goals and enemies. Fragmentation is fragmentation, whether class versus class or street versus street. The problem with both types of warfare is that while each side retains an acute understanding of morality, it does not extend that understanding to the other side. This violates any type of balance between resistance and achievement. There is in such a discourse no balance between existence and control.

According to Shakur, the gang warfare in Los Angeles sought control for no other purpose than control. When drugs where introduced into the environment, they quickly became the focus of control. It is only when an alternative focus (Black Nationalism as the original focus of the gang activity) is introduced into the environment that existence becomes a moderating factor upon control and the balance between resistance and achievement is restored. The irony is that in no other discourse besides the romantic golden age has this Black utopian vision been somewhat understood and articulated. The truth that we must find in this vision is that all components of a community exhibit moderating influences upon the other components. If Monster teaches us anything, it should teach us the importance of community and visions of community.

One of the most essential problems in south-central Los Angeles, as in many other Black communities across the United States in the post–Civil Rights era, was that no real vision of community existed. It may not be a coincidence that during the period when gang activity began to develop at an alarming rate, the jeremiad was busying itself with developing individual conceptions of achievement, such as that proffered by Shelby Steele. The act of Black middle-class distancing from inner-city communities left such communities vulnerable. Because one can see the sanctity of community in the early, predrug gang activity, one can envision such activity as the worst articulation of justice, the worst attempt to implement a system of justice from within the community.

Our need for visions of community upon which to found justice are essential; Kelley and our youth are correct in their faith that these visions must be grounded in a studied reality. Beyond all the mechanics of justice, justice is in all communities the balance between resistance and achievement, the balance between existence and control, the balance between individual and collective will. To forget that balance, as evidenced by middle-class flight from Black communities, which placed a premium on individualism and control, is to invite immaturity into the void.

Granted, we cannot ignore the danger of visions and political systems built upon visions. I do not argue that such species are not dangerous; instead I argue that they are fundamental. On the other hand, the critiques of Kelley against this "golden" vision, Socrates' critique of Athenian democracy, Malcolm X's critique of U.S. democracy and various other societal critiques are equally fundamental. The problem is that the visionaries can never divorce themselves from contradictory baggage—they are never willing to hear alternative voices. In the case of Black visions, the voice speaks against romantic naiveté, a sort of exaggerated nostalgia and fallacious beginnings.

Still, the vision is mature in a way we have yet to perceive. It posits justice derived from resistance upon a communal level, in fact, justice derived from the very struggle Kelley in his work lauds. Forms of democracy, no matter how radical they appear, cannot function or develop without understandings and visions of justice. In fact, as our analysis of achievement and resistance informs us, resistance must balance and be balanced by achievement—that is the vision most Black people in the United States share, across all three traditions. While oppositional struggle strengthens Black resistance, Black achievement depends on attempts to articulate a systematic vision of the foundations upon which political systems and societies develop—what Dubois argues as the fulfillment of Black genius. In other words, our psyche, our very identity as a unique culture, and the fulfillment of our individual identities within that context, are dependent upon our ability to fully develop both components, resistance and achievement, within the political context and then to counterbalance achievement with understandings of resistance.

Black people within the United States, indeed within the entire Diaspora, have resisted dehumanization for well over three centuries. Kelley's work, among others, posits that this resistance has been incorporated into cultural traditions, indeed has become systematic on a fundamental level. This argument envisions three hundred years of experience of analyzing and critiquing understandings of justice. The immediate need is to universalize those understandings within the context of Black culture. A coercive system need not exist to enforce such understandings; indeed the lack of systematic coercion adds to the dynamic context in which any system of justice must emerge and operate. In such a context perhaps the critiques of Kelley and others will not merely be tolerated but truly heard and understood. At any rate, philosophy has inherited the job of universalizing three centuries of resistive experiences into an understanding of justice.

Broad-Based Black Leadership

An essential goal of mediation is that of tuning down the voices in the conflict between the Black jeremiad and Black Nationalism so that these voices do not continue to drown out other voices in the Black community and also so these traditions can hear other voices besides their own. To achieve this, Black cultural pluralism must develop. That development is centered in amalgamation, adaptation, inclusiveness and improvisation. Essential to that development is the development of institutions of cultural pluralism that can reconstruct the strength of Black spiritualism, develop a functional balance between resistance and achievement, and develop a discourse of justice founded upon the history of the Black community.

There is a story to be told in the life experience of El-Hajj Malik El-Shabazz. That story lies in his political journey, a journey that takes most of the thirty-nine years of his life span. During the span of that journey he is able to transit within and beyond nearly every political venue within the Black community and help to develop at least two political traditions—Black Nationalism and Black cultural pluralism. In fact, El-Hajj Malik El-Shabazz stands, in the last years of his life, as transited beyond the constraints of Black Nationalism, as the only national leader of Black cultural pluralism. Indeed cultural pluralists see in Malik El-Shabazz, as evidenced by Kelley's analysis, the ability to successfully articulate Black narratives and the hidden transcript on the political level within a dynamic national political context.

In him we envision that same Black excellence that we reconstructed in Douglass and our young Haitian rebel who teaches his fellow rebels how to die by positioning his body more in the fire and enduring in silence. Not the excellence to die for a cause, even though we laud that in others and secretly seek it within ourselves, but the excellence to focus in themselves and others their will to resist. Malik El-Shabazz, above most other Black leaders with maybe the noted exception of Douglass, exhibited this same excellence. He exhibited it in his ability to speak to a wide spectrum of African peoples and Europeans and articulate to them the terms of Black resistance.

The most salient feature of that excellence stands as his ability to move beyond the constraints of Black Nationalism. In transiting beyond, Malik El-Shabazz achieved that which no Black leader of his stature achieved: the ability to focus Black excellence in achievement. In the attempt to develop the Organization of Afro-American Unity, he transited beyond Black Nationalism in his attempt to link with other Black organizations; he also reconstructed Black Nationalism within the context of achievement that was so essential to Garvey's Black Nationalism, but had gotten lost in the Nation of Islam's institutional agenda.

Malik El-Shabazz's leadership is the template upon which broad-based leadership needs to be based. Grounded in the community, broad-based leadership must also seek, develop and maintain balance both between individual interests and community interests, and between resistance and achievement. Reputation, power, politics and money by themselves do not retain the ability to mire the Black community in stasis. It is how we, especially Black leaders, pursue each that is essential. We can choose to pursue them within the context of community, in which lie particular constraints, and in that choice we can develop a discourse that sets the parameters of those constraints, or we can choose to pursue these things outside of our community. Each choice affects our ability to end the stasis within our community, and each of us is aware of our choices.

Notes

Chapter One

1. Du Bois, 1903: 6.
2. Kinney, 2001.
3. Levine, 1977: 239.
4. Levine, 1977: 153
5. Hord and Lee, 1995: 5.
6. Douglass, 1986: 78–79.
7. As an alternative to mainstream "static" philosophy, there are academics who argue, and reasonably so, that philosophies are "products of time, place and situation, and thus systems of timed history rather than timeless eternity." It has also been argued that fundamental principles, values and understandings of a particular political system must be a dominant part of people's political culture *before* they can be institutionalized. See Alain Locke, "Values and Imperatives," in *Philosophy Born of Struggle* (Leonard Harris, ed.); and Ian Morris, "The Strong Principle of Equality and the Archaic Origins of Greek Democracy" in *Demokratia* (Ober and Hedrick, eds.).
8. Green, 2001: 72–74.
9. Dover, 1974: 232.
10. Dover, 1974: 232.
11. Douglass, 1845: 58.
12. Douglass, 1845: 115.
13. Du Bois, 1903: 5.
14. Appiah, 1992: 32.
15. Cruse, 1967: 13–14.

16. Levine, 1977: 153
17. Kelley, 1994: 8.

Chapter Two

1. Levine, 1977: 32–33.
2. Berger, 1969: 15.
3. Commentators from other cultures, such as Henry Kim, have attributed the political energy of the Black community to experience gained during the Civil Rights movement and/or the boldness of the Black Power movement that followed. Such commentators have taken what appears to be a snapshot of Black culture and retain understandings insufficient to envision the degree of political thought and development required to produce both movements.
4. Levine, 1977: 3–5.
5. Concerning this point, we have agreement from most Black scholars including scholars as disparate as Levine, West and Kelley.
6. Douglass, 1845: 51.
6. Douglass, 1845: 51.
8. Douglass, 1845: 52.
9. Gordon, 1997: 274.
10. Douglass, 1845: 47.
11. Douglass, 1845: 48–49.
12. Douglass, 1845: 72–73.
13. Douglass, 1845: 72.
14. Berlin, 132–134. Franklin, 1984: 71.
15. Grandy, 1843: 7–8.
16. Douglass, 1845: 111.
17. Douglass, 1845: 57–58.
18. Douglass, 1845: 58.
19. Levine, 1977: 34
20. Douglass, 1845: 75.
21. Douglass, 1845: 111–114.
22. Gordon, 1997: 273–290.
23. Fouchard, Jean, 1972 [1981]: 103.
24. Again the exceptions would be nihilism and anarchy, neither of which can be shown to have existed for any significant moment or within any significant space within human memory.
25. Campbell, 1988: 34.
26. Campbell, Fouchard, Giddings and others all report how slaves were rewarded for capturing and killing Maroons and how Maroon communities often raided plantations for enlistees, especially females.
27. Robinson, 1997: 13.
28. Fouchard, Jean, 1972 [1981]: 117.
29. Campbell, 1988: 34.
30. James, 1963: 276.
31. James, 1963: 361.
32. Campbell, 1988: 35.

33. Campbell, 1988: 35.
34. Grant, 1973: 259–260.
35. Grant, 1973: 261.
36. James, 1963: 19.
37. James, 1963: 276.
39. James, 1963: 361.
39. James, 1963: 315.
40. James, 1963: 361.
41. James, 1963: 256.
42. James, 1963: 393.
43. James, 1963: 19.
44. James, 1963: 20–22, 86–88, 96.
45. James, 1963: 82–130.
46. Nicholls, 1979: 35.
47. Nicholls, 1979: 38.
48. Nicholls, 1979: 36.
49. Kellye, 1994: 161. Original source for quote: *Negro Digest* 1, no. 4 (Winter–Spring, 1943), 301.
50. Douglass, 1845: 149–150.
51. Robinson, 1997: 51.
52. Henry, 1990: 60. Levine, 1977: 30–34. Howard-Pitney, 1986: 481–492.
53. Howard-Pitney, 1986: 482.
54. Howard-Pitney, 1986: 482–483.
55. Levy, 1992: 12.
56. Howard-Pitney, 1986: 483.
57. Howard-Pitney, 1986: 483.
58. Henry, 1990: 61.
59. Howard-Pitney, 1986: 483.
60. Porter, 1995: 358.
61. Robinson, 1997: 47–48.
62. Robinson, 1997: 48.
63. Robinson, 1997: 48.
64. Boxill, 1997: 273–274.
65. Robinson, 1997: 51–52.
66 Du Bois, 1903: 42
67. Boxill, 1997: 275, 288–290.
68. Boxill, 1997: 276.
69. Boxill, 1997: 279–281.
70. Boxill, 1997: 282–284.
71. Boxill, 1997: 290.
72. Boxill, 1997: 284–285.
73. Boxill, 1997: 285.
74. James, 1963: 361.
75. Douglass, 1845: 103–105.
76. Douglass, 1845: 114.
77. Douglass, 1855: 279–280.
78.. Campbell, 1988: 34.

79. Douglass, 1845: 110–111.
80. Douglass, 1994: 281.
81. Nash, 1989: 333.
82. Nash, 1989: 335.
83. Nash, 1989: 336.
84. Nash, 1989: 337.
85. Dawson, 2001: 17.
86. Porter, 1995: 249.
87. As most commentators on the question assert, free Blacks began to strongly oppose the American Colonization Society that was formed in 1817. The Colonization Society formed around a coalition of Northern clergy, Northern and Southern white philanthropists concerned about free Blacks in the United States, and Southern slave owners concerned about their ability to maintain the institution of slavery in the United States. The first formal organizing meeting, December 21, 1816, at the Davis Hotel in Washington D.C., included the following attendees: James Monroe, Bushrod Washington, Andrew Jackson, Francis Scott Key, Daniel Webster, with Henry Clay presiding. Given the coalition of interests, free Blacks suspected the Colonization Society's efforts as being strongly self-interested with the main interest being to push free Blacks out of the United States.
88. Delany, 1968: 30–31.
89. Porter, 1995: 303.
90. Porter, 1995: 257.
91. Porter, 1995: 290–291.

Chapter Three

1. Slave legend from Solomon Legare Island (South Carolina) as told by Ms. Phyllis Green, in *The American Slave: A Composite Autobiography*, volume 11, George P. Rawick (ed.), 1977: 179.
2. Green, 2001: 71.
3. Vlastos, 1994: 103.
4. Green, 2001: 72.
5. Hedrick and Ober, 1996: 20.
6. Hedrick and Ober, 1996: 20.
7. Douglass, 1855: 57–58.
8. Du Bois, 1903: 5.
9. Levine, 1977: 32–33.
10. Levine, 1977: 78.
11. Douglass, 1850: 58.
12. Douglass, 1845: 57.
13. Levine, 1977: 134.
14. Levine, 1977: 174.
15. Levine, 1977: 175.
16. Washington, 1974: 586.
17. Washington, 1974: 585.
18. Levine, 1977: 176.
19. Levine, 1977: 176.
20. Levine, 1977: 239.

21. Kelley, 1994: 44–45.
22. Du Bois, 1903: 40.
23. Levine, 1977: 217.
24. Levine, 1977: 217.
25. In his work, *Plural But Equal*, Cruse recognized this phenomenon in his analysis of the failure of the United States to properly implement the *Brown v. Board* decision.
26. Jones, 1963: 27.
27. Levine, 1977: 7–8.
28. Jones, 1963: 27.
29. Couto, 1993: 71.
30. Kelley, 1994: 49.
31. Jones, 1963: 27–28.
32. Levine, 1977: 195.
33. Jones, 1963: 27.
34. Levine, 1977: 177.
35. Levine, 1977: 177.
36. Levine, 1977: 200.
37. Levine, 1977: 200.
38. Levine, 1977: 201.
39. Levine, 1977: 237.
40. Levine, 1977: 237.
41. Kelley: 1997. See chapter Eight, "Kickin' Reality, Kickin Ballistics: "Gangsta Rap" and Postindustrial Los Angeles, 185–227.
42. Du Bois, 1903: 5.

Chapter Four

1. Du Bois, 1903: 40.
2. Thucydides, (2.39–2.41)
3. Porter, 1995: 88–89.
4. Porter, 1995: 417.
5. Howard-Pitney, 1986: 491.
6. Porter, 1995: 293.
7. Porter, 1995: 296.
8. Washington, 1965: 37.
9. Du Bois, 1903: 36–37.
10. Washington, September 1895. Speech given at Cotton States and International Exposition, Atlanta Georgia.
11. Du Bois, 1903: 72.
12. Du Bois, 1903: 42
13. Du Bois, 1903: 43.
14. Du Bois, 1903: 43.
15. Washington, 1974: 583.
16. Washington, 1974: 585–586.
17. Du Bois, 1903: 38.

18. Du Bois. 1903: 42.

19. Du Bois,1903: 209.

20. Robinson, 1997: 1.

21. Fouchard, 1972: 103.

22. Nicholls, 1979: 35.

23. Nicholls, 1979: 38.

24. Moses, 1982: 127–129.

25. Moses, 1982: 125, 129; Dawson, 2001: 90–131.

26. Moses, 1982: 127.

27. Jones 1963: 61.

28. Jones 1963: 79.

29. Jones 1963: 80.

30. Wintz, 1996: 216

31. Garvey, 1967: 58.

32. Moses, 1982: 133.

33. Essien-Udom and Garvey, 1977: 134.

34. Garvey, 1967: 33.

35. Garvey, 1967: 33.

36. Garvey, 1967: xvi.

37. Garvey, 1967: 32–33.

38. Kelley, 2002: 27.

39. Reed, 1999: 201.

40. Kelley, 1994: 180.

41. Kelley, 1994: 181.

42. Kelley, 1994: 162.

43. Kelley, 2002: 23–29.

44. Kelley, 1994: 8.

45. Kelley, 1994: 8.

46. Fogelson, 1967: 338.

47. Fogelson, 1967: 364.

48. Harris, 1998: 368–385.

49. Henry, 1990: 54.

50. Olzak, Shanahan & McEneaney, 1996: 609.

51. Olzak, Shanahan & McEneaney, 1996: 608.

52. James, 1963: 19.

53. James, 1963: 20–22, 86–88, 96.

54. Levine, 1977: 153

55. Levine, 1977: 163.

56. Cruse, 1967: 13–14.

57. Kelley, 1997: 165.

58. Kelley, 1997: 166.

59. Kelley, 1997: 169.

60. Kelley, 1997: 170.

61. Cruse, 1967: 7–8.

62. Henry, 1990: 37.

63. I first began to think of Black cultural pluralism as a distinct tradition within Black political

thought exactly because of the development of Black narratives and the hidden transcript. Neither of the other two traditions had ever had need for the hidden transcript during their development (except maybe Black Nationalists held in bondage), yet both institutions have endured into the present.

64. Levine, 1977: 367–440.

Chapter Five

1. Cruse, 1967: 5–6.
2. Du Bois, 1903: 5.
3. West, 1994: 25.
4. See Kelley's last two chapters of *Race Rebels*. Kelley develops the street as the site of Black masculinity and resistance to oppression through the life of Malcolm X and West Coast *gangsta rap*. Also see Lubiano's "Black Nationalism and Black Common Sense," in *The House That Race Built*, 1998: 232–252.
5. Steele, 1991: 95–96.
6. Marable, 1983: 200.
7. Marable, 1983: 208.
8. Robinson, 1997: 144.
9. Marable, 1983: 196.
10. Steele, 1991: 96.
11. Farrakhan, 1993.
12. Dawson, 2001.
13. Kelley 1997: 6–7.

Chapter Six

1. Gordon, 1997: 5–7.
2. Hord and Lee, 1995: 5.
3. Hord and Lee, 1995: 6.
4. I use the word "philosophy" here somewhat for convenience. Obviously I do not mean just those scholars trained in the Western tradition of philosophy. Writers who appear in Black philosophical editions operate from a variety of academic and nonacademic disciplines. The other side of the coin is that Black philosophy has always been political. And one could and does argue that politics without philosophy makes bad politics, and philosophy without politics makes bad philosophy. See Green, 2001; and Euben, 1991.
5. Kelley 1994: 210.
6. Hord and Lee, 1995: 6.
7. Hord and Lee, 1995: 6.
8. Du Bois, 1903: 12.
9. Shakur, 1993: 382–383.
10. Kelley, 1994: 39.

Bibliography

Appiah, Kwame (1992). *In My Father's House: Africa in the Philosophy of Culture*. New York: Oxford University Press.

Berger, Bennett (1995). *An Essay on Culture: Symbolic Structure and Social Structure*. Berkeley: University of California Press.

Berlin, Ira, Marc Favreau and Steven F. Miller (Eds.) (c.1988). *Remembering Slavery: African Americans Talk about Their Personal Experiences of Slavery and Freedom*. New York: The New Press; Washington, D.C.: in association with The Library of Congress.

Boxill, Bernard (1997). "The Fight with Covey." *Existence in Black*, 273–290. New York: Routledge.

Campbell, Mavis (1988). "Maroons of the Caribbean." *NACLA Report on the Americas* 25, 4 (February): 34–37.

Couto, Richard (1993). "Narrative, Free Space and Political Leadership in Social Movements." *The Journal of Politics* 55, 1 (Fall): 57–79.

Cruse, Harold (1967). *The Crisis of the Negro Intellectual*. New York: Quill.

Cruse, Harold (1987). *Plural but Equal: A Critical Study of Blacks and Minorities and America's Plural Society*. New York: Quill.

Dawson, Michael (2001). *Black Visions: The Roots of Contemporary African-American Political Ideologies*. Chicago and London: University of Chicago Press.

Delany, Martin (1968). *The Condition, Elevation, Emigration, and Destiny of the Colored People of the United States*. New York: Arno Press.

Douglass, Frederick (1845). *Narrative of the Life of Frederick Douglass: An American Slave*. Reprinted with an introduction by Houston A. Baker, Jr. New York: Penguin Books, 1986.

Douglass, Frederick (1994). *The Autobiographies*. New York: Library of America.

Dover, K.J. (1974). *Greek Popular Morality in the Time of Plato and Aristotle*. Berkeley and Los Angeles: University of California Press.

Du Bois, W.E.B. (1903). *The Souls of Black Folk*. Reprinted with introduction by Donald B. Gibson. New York: Penguin Classics, 1989.

Essien-Udom, E.U., and Amy J. Garvey (Eds.) (1977). *More Philosophy and Opinions of Marcus Garvey*. London: Cass.

Euben, Peter, J. "Socrates in America," *Salmagundi*, 92, Fall (1991): 211–225.

Farrakhan, Louis (1993). "The Role of Leadership in Uniting Africa and Black America." *Final Call*, 12, 16 (Jan. 16).

Fogelson, Robert (1967). "White on Black: A Critique of the McCone Commission Report on the Los Angeles Riots." *Political Science Quarterly*, 82, 3 (Sept.): 337–367.

Fouchard, Jean (1972). *The Haitian Maroons: Liberty or Death*. Trans. by A. Faulkner Watts. New York: Edward W. Blyden Press, 1981.

Garvey, Amy J. (Ed.) (1967). *Philosophy and Opinions of Marcus Garvey*. London.

Gordon, Lewis. (Ed.) (1997). *Existence in Black*. New York: Routledge.

Grandy, Moses (1843). *Narrative of the Life of Moses Grandy*. Electronic Edition, Http://docsouth.unc.edu/grandy/grandy accessed March, 2004, Chapel Hill, (1996).

Grant, John (1973). "Black Immigration into Nova Scotia 1176–1815." *Journal of Negro History*, 58, 3 (July): 253–270.

Green, Ricky (c. 2001). *Democratic Virtue in the Trial and Death of Socrates: Resistance to Imperialism in Classical Athens*. New York: Peter Lang.

Harris, Daryl (1998). "The Logic of Black Urban Rebellions." *Journal of Black Studies*, 28, 3 (Jan.): 368–385.

Harris, Leonard. (Ed.) (1983). *Philosophy Born of Struggle: Anthology of Afro-American Philosophy from 1917*. Dubuque, Iowa: Kendall Hunt.

Henry, Charles (1990). *Culture and African American Politics*. Bloomington: Indiana University Press.

Hord, Fred, and Jonathan Lee (Eds.) (1995). *I Am Because We Are: Readings in Black Philosophy*. Amherst: University of Massachusetts Press.

Howard-Pitney, David (1986). "The Enduring Black Jeremiad: The American Jeremiad and Black Protest Rhetoric, from Frederick Douglass to W.E.B. Du Bois, 1841–1919, *American Quarterly*, 38, 3: 481–492.

James, C.L.R. (1963). *The Black Jacobins: Toussaint L'Ouverture and the San Domingo Revolution*. New York: Vintage Books.

Jones, Leroi (1963). *Blues People: Negro Music in White America*: Edinburgh: MacGibbon and Kee.

Kelley, Robin. (1994). *Race Rebels: Culture, Politics and the Black Working Class*. New York: The Free Press.

Kelley, Robin (2002). *Freedom Dreams: The Black Radical Imagination*. Boston: Beacon Press.

Kinney, T. (2001). "Black Youth Demand Change in Cincinnati." *The California Advocate*, 34,15 (April 20).

Levine, Lawrence (1977). *Black Culture and Black Consciousness: Afro-American Folk Thought from Slavery to Freedom*. New York: Oxford University Press.

Levy, Michael B. (Ed.) (c. 1992). *Political Thought in America: An Anthology*. Prospect Heights, Illinois: Waveland Press.

Lubiano, Wahneema. (Ed.) (1998). *The House That Race Built: Original Essays by Toni Morrison, Angela Y. Davis, Cornel West, and Others on Black Americans and Politics in America Today*. New York: Vintage Books.

Marable, Manning (1983). *How Capitalism Underdeveloped Black America: Problems in Race, Political Economy and Society*. Boston: South End Press.

Moses, Wilson (1982). *Black Messiahs and Uncle Toms: Social and Literary Manipulations of a Religious Myth*. Philadelphia: Pennsylvania State University Press.

Nash, Gary (1989). "New Light on Richard Allen: The Early Years of Freedom." *William and Mary Quarterly*, Third Series, 46, 2 (April): 332–340.

Nicholls, David (1979). *From Dessalines to Duvalier: Race, Colour and National Independence in Haiti*. New York: Cambridge University Press.

Ober, Josiah and Charles Hedrick (Eds.) (1996). *Demokratia: A Conversation on Democracies, Ancient and Modern*. Princeton, NJ: Princeton University Press.

Olzak, Susan, Elizabeth Shanahan and Elizabeth McEneaney (1996). "Poverty, Segregation, and Race Riots: 1960 to 1993." *American Sociological Review*, 61, 4 (August): 590–613.

Porter, Dorothy (1995). *Early Negro Writing*. Baltimore: Black Classic Press.

Rawick, George (1977). *The American Slave: A Composite Autobiography*, Westport, Connecticut: Greenwood Publishing.

Reed, Alfred (1999). *Stirrings in the Jug: Black Politics in the Post-Segregation Era*. Minneapolis and London: University of Minnesota Press.

Robinson, Cedric (1983). *Black Marxism: The Making of the Black Radical Tradition*. London: Zed Books.

Robinson, Cedric (1997). *Black Movements in America*. New York and London: Routledge.

Shakur, Sanyika (1993). *Monster: The Autobiography of an L.A. Gang Member*. New York: Penguin Books.

Sowell, Thomas (1987). *A Conflict of Visions: Ideological Origins of Political Struggles*. New York: Quill.

Sowell, Thomas (1990). *Preferential Policies: An International Perspective*. New York: William Morrow.

Steele, Shelby (1991). *The Content of Our Character: A New Vision of Race in America*. New York: Harper Perennial.

Thucydides. *History of the Peloponnesian War*. Translated by Rex Warner, with an introduction and notes by M. I. Finley. Harmondsworth, Eng., and Baltimore: Penguin Books 1972.

Vlastos, Gregory (1994). *Socratic Studies*. Cambridge: Cambridge University Press.

Washington, Booker (1965). *Three Negro Classics: Up from Slavery / Booker T. Washington; The Souls of Black Folk / William E.B. Dubois; The Autobiography of an Ex-Colored Man / James Weldon Johnson*. New York: Avon Books.

Washington, Booker T. (1974). *The Booker T. Washington Papers: Volume 3: 1889–1895*. Edited by Louis Harlan. Urbana, Chigago and London: University of Illinois Press.

West, Cornell (1993). *Keeping Faith*. New York: Routledge.

West, Cornell (1994). *Race Matters*. New York: Vintage Books.

Williams-Myers, A.J. (1996). "Slavery, Rebellion, and Revolution in the Americas." *Journal of Black Studies*, 26, 4 (March): 381–400.

Wintz, Cary (Ed.) (c.1996). *African American Political Thought, 1890–1930*. New York: M.E. Sharpe.

Index

U

V

W

AFRICAN AMERICAN LITERATURE AND CULTURE

EXPANDING AND EXPLODING THE BOUNDARIES

General Editor
Carlyle V. Thompson

The purpose of this series is to present innovative, in-depth, and provocatively critical literary and cultural investigations of critical issues in African American literature and life. We welcome critiques of fiction, poetry, drama, film, sports, and popular culture. Of particular interest are literary and cultural analyses that involve contemporary psychoanalytical criticism, new historicism, deconstructionism, critical race theory, critical legal theory, and critical gender theory.

For additional information about this series or for the submission of manuscripts, please contact:

Peter Lang Publishing, Inc.
Acquisitions Department
275 Seventh Avenue, 28th floor
New York, New York 10001

To order other books in this series, please contact our Customer Service Department:

(800) 770-LANG (within the U.S.)
(212) 647-7706 (outside the U.S.)
(212) 647-7707 FAX

Or browse online by series:

www.peterlangusa.com